Psychology for Architects

ARCHITECTURAL SCIENCE SERIES

Editor

HENRY J. COWAN

Professor of Architectural Science
University of Sydney

Psychology
for
Architects

by

DAVID CANTER
Ph.D., A.B.Ps.S., A.I.J.

University of Surrey, England

APPLIED SCIENCE PUBLISHERS LTD

LONDON

APPLIED SCIENCE PUBLISHERS LTD
RIPPLE ROAD, BARKING, ESSEX, ENGLAND

ISBN: 0 85334 590 2

WITH 5 TABLES AND 26 ILLUSTRATIONS
© APPLIED SCIENCE PUBLISHERS LTD 1974

Printed in Great Britain by Galliard (Printers) Ltd Great Yarmouth

Preface

Science fiction and the not so fictitious history of the effects of scientific discovery have led many to fear the expanding influence of scientists. This fear is no more apparent than in the realm of architecture. Yet many of the weaknesses in present day design can be traced to inhibitions which derive from erroneous assumptions about human behaviour. A fuller, clearer and more scientific understanding of people should help free architecture from these inhibitions and give rise to buildings which are both more satisfying for their users and greater works of art. The central aim of this book is to lay the foundations for such an understanding.

Two key assumptions (or acts of faith) are central to the approach behind this book. Firstly, it has been assumed that psychology has a very broad relevance for architects. From this viewpoint the environment they manipulate has been taken to cover as wide a perspective as possible, including for instance, spatial and visual aspects as well as those aspects usually considered such as lighting or acoustic levels. The consideration of the actual process of producing the environment has also been taken as an important area of architectural research which will benefit from psychology.

The second assumption is that human behaviour in buildings is open to scientific study. The ways in which science works are discussed at various points throughout the book, but the arguments in favour of a scientific approach are not spelt out in great detail. The main reason for this is that the same assumptions which make architecture possible give rise to the possibilities for scientific study of people in buildings. For, if human behaviour was so erratic or unpredictable that it was impossible to find principles which underlay it, or to discover trends within it, then it would never be possible for one person to produce buildings for others to use, because he would never know what to expect of the users nor they of him. That the profession of architecture has been active with some degree of success for many centuries is thus strong evidence that it should be possible to develop a scientific psychology for architects.

This is not a textbook. It is instead a book which might be read either before or in conjunction with a textbook. It provides an account of the basic psychological concepts which are relevant to the practice of architecture, or which are necessary for the comprehension of that research carried out with the aim of contributing directly to decisions about the built environment.

Anyone wishing simply to gain a broad understanding of the great majority of topics of which present day psychology consists should not look for that understanding in this book, but in one of the wide range of excellent introductory textbooks which are readily available. Neither is this a detailed account of the research which psychologists have undertaken in order to assist design decision making. Aspects of that research are touched upon and it is briefly reviewed in an appendix. The detailed examination which such a topic demands will form a separate book.

Unlike a textbook this book takes an obvious stand on various issues in psychology. From time to time I have been prepared to put aside the author's omniscient invisibility and to write in the first person, expressing opinions. One reason for this was that in such a brief book it facilitates clarity of exposition. However, a more powerful reason was to assist with my didactic mission. Experience with architects and architectural students has indicated to me that interest is generated more readily by firmly expressed opinions than by bland statements. They give the audience some standpoint against which to react and thus motivate a search for understanding, if only to attack the opinions the more readily. A third reason was that, at this early stage in linking psychology and architecture, any author of a general book must select his material without the help of a generally accepted viewpoint to assist with this selection. Thus, to hide the fact that the selections made are not inevitable, and to pretend that the approaches which emerge follow some professional consensus, would be to take an unfair advantage of the ignorance of my readers. By showing my hand I hope that readers will be more prepared to consider the issues for themselves and try to discover other viewpoints. (The specific references in the chapters or the general references at the end of each chapter are there to facilitate this.)

Most chapters begin with an example which, it is intended, should be used through group discussions (or by personal consideration) to generate questions about the issues presented and thus to encourage a search outside of this book. Some questions are given at the end of each chapter to initiate the discussion and it will be found that considerations beyond those within the chapter will be necessary to answer these questions. Similarly there are some rather obvious gaps in the areas of psychology, or in the psychologists referred to, in this book. These gaps are usually there because it was felt that the work was both readily accessible in a comprehensible form to non-psychologists and/or required the sort of detailed discussion to draw out its relevance that was not possible in so short a book. At the back of my mind there was also often a feeling that some of these 'obvious' areas of psychology provide something of a cul-de-sac for architects.

In part, this book is an attempt to counteract the tendency, amongst some psychologists, of using scientific terminology (some would say, jargon) without being fully prepared to explain its meaning to the layman. Nor have they drawn together the strings of research by different workers into a form coherent enough to be comprehensible to the noviciate. In effect they have helped to turn psychology into a mystery and reduce its general availability to the interested layman. The chapters which follow are aimed at removing some of this mystification and to act as a link to more traditional psychological texts.

Finally, I would like to express my thanks to all the people who have, over the years, entered into discussion with me on the issues covered in this book. Though many of them will be surprised to learn it, their questioning, or uncomprehending silence, has been the most important impetus to the production of this book.

I am particularly grateful to Peter Manning, Tom Markus and Terence Lee, each of whom, in succession, has given me the encouragement and the environment in which to explore this field. Ross Thorne gave me valuable comments on the book as a whole.

Harry McGurk, Russell Wicks, Ian Davies and Stephen Tagg have all commented in detail on specific chapters. I thank them all. The forbearance, efficiency and speed with which Jean Donohoe, Rosalind Gilbert and Jenny Buisson each typed parts of the various drafts is also gratefully acknowledged.

Mike Leigh, with the assistance of Tom Ottar, provided the illustrations. For their considerable success in clarifying, and at the same time commenting upon, the text I am sure the reader will wish to thank them as much as I do.

The importance of my wife's role as a personal and professional super-ego cannot be over-estimated. Any qualities which the book has I owe to her.

DAVID CANTER
Surrey

Contents

Chapter 1

By Way of Introduction

1.1. The Widening Gap

In writing about Mies van der Rohe in *The Observer* on 24th August, 1969 the Smithsons had this to say:

'Two separate but reciprocal themes emerge: an almost autonomous repetitive neutralising skin; and an open-space-structured building-recessive, a calm, green, urban pattern. Together they are Mies's immortality.'

Contrast that statement with the following from the *Daily Mail* (10th October) of the same year:

'The builders were delighted when their new housing scheme received a commendation for its design and they were surprised when the local town council could find no volunteer to attend the unveiling ceremony.

They were really shaken when members of the council described the scheme as a "monstrosity" and compared it with a tribal village in darkest Africa.'

And contrast *that* with the quotation which *The Observer* (10th August 1969) attributed to a psychiatrist:

'Half the mental hospitals would be empty and psychiatrists out of a job if every home had two bathrooms and soundproof bedrooms.'

Taken at their face value these three quotations illustrate in different ways the desperate need which there now is for fundamental psychological information to be fed into the design process. The quotation from the Smithsons epitomises the abstract visual orientation of much thinking in architecture and contrasts markedly with the medical opinion of the psychiatrist. Yet even within this visual discipline the language and concepts are neither available to the

1

uninitiated nor particularly clear to the cognoscenti. The quotation from the *Daily Mail* highlights the recurring problem that many people do not seem to think as highly of buildings as the design professions do themselves. The psychiatrist's statement illustrates the widespread belief that changes in society and the quality of life are in many cases not in a positive direction and that in some situations design developments may actually be aggravating social and psychological stress. Central to all of these issues is the number of different people involved in producing buildings. For instance, it is just conceivable that these three quotations could have been made in reference to the same group of buildings! But even though that was not the case they illustrate the wide gulf that there is between the variety of approaches which exist towards buildings.

That this gap is widening can be further illustrated by considering, say, for example, a commercial office block. There will be the finance company which provides the money and whose concern will be with the economic viability of the project. There will be the development company which, although commercially oriented, will be more directly concerned with the ease of letting offices. There will probably be a more or less separate group concerned with managing the building and which, of course, will be conscious of the ease with which administrative and security processes can be carried out. The local authority, and in many cases central government, will also be involved in decisions about the building. At the bottom of this pile of people and organisations are those we may refer to as 'the building users'.

The 'user' group will itself be very diverse. Within the organisation they will range from middle-aged men in senior management to teenage girls carrying out repetitive clerical tasks. Besides these people who regularly work within the building there will be 'users' who visit the building, and people within it, for various lengths of time with different degrees of frequency. Finally there are those who use the building in the sense that they arrange to meet people at its entrance; simply look at it as they pass by; use it as a landmark as they move around the city, or indeed have just heard of it as a strange example of modern architecture.

On the one hand the various groups of administrators will have a variety of opinions about the building and how it might affect people. On the other hand the various users will react to or be influenced by the building in a variety of ways. How can the issues involved in all this be resolved?

1.2. The Bridge of Scientific Psychology

Clearly there is no simple answer to this complex problem but an important start may be made by examining the issue central to all the above considerations. This is the way in which the physical environment influences people and the ways in which they in turn influence it.

For instance the Smithsons' comments on Mies van der Rohe are an attempt to show the way in which the formal visual properties of his buildings influence the reactions of users. Their explanation illustrates the way in which some architects have dealt with these problems by creating an esoteric, private language within which there is no possibility of providing evidence to test statements. How can we ever know, for example, if the 'skin' is 'neutralising' or not.

The difficulty which the builders had in understanding the reactions of the council members could also be related to psychological considerations. Both groups clearly had quite different conceptions of what the buildings were meant to be. One group was probably concerned with the judgements people had made of what it looked like, the other with the actual effects of the buildings on what people did. Once again we have the difficulty that both groups have their own opinions and there is little possibility of either clarifying these or putting them to any test other than the strength with which they are held.

The psychiatrist's opinion looks on the face of it more acceptable as a basis for common understanding and decision making. We are not talking about 'darkest Africa' or any such easily misunderstood abstraction but about numbers of hospital beds and bathrooms. However, the underlying assumptions are still about the way buildings affect people. Yet it is unlikely that the psychiatrist in question (with his medical background) has anything other than anecdotal evidence to go on. His concern no doubt was with the well-being of his patients rather than trying to lay down any general principles which could be widely applied. His statement is really a summary of the problems he himself had experienced and as such forms an intriguing basis for an hypothesis to be tested by the methods of scientific psychology.

Interestingly enough some of the communications with others, for instance with the local authority or the people responsible for maintaining standards laid down in building regulations, will in fact be discussions about the psychological implications of design decisions. This is so because many building regulations, if not actually based on psychological research, are based directly upon assumptions about the psychological impact of building forms. For instance, to use the window example, the daylight regulations which most countries have relate to assumptions about how people will react given various amounts of daylight.

There are two points being illustrated here. First, that a great deal of the discussion and many of the decisions made in relation to buildings are based upon assumptions about people and their interactions with buildings. Secondly that it is only when these relationships are expressed and understood in the context of scientific psychology that communication amongst decision makers, and the actual decisions made, can *develop* in an effective and meaningful way.

Clearly psychology is not the whole answer to these issues but it is a crucial part of such an answer. The aim of this book is to lay the groundwork upon which the relevant psychological facts and concepts can be based. Exactly what is meant by a scientific psychological approach is examined in some detail in Chapter 2.

1.3. Frequent Assumptions

To illustrate further the central role of psychological assumptions in building design, let us consider some of the issues which will be examined more fully in later chapters.

In designing a building most architects are constantly involved in what the building looks like. In effect this means that they are trying to create a physical form which will be perceived in a particular set of ways. For instance, to exaggerate the perceived volume of an interior he may specify that the walls should be light blue or he might make the roofs of houses sloping so that people will 'see' them as more homely. Then again he might feel that he had created 'a calm, green, urban pattern' which required some 'reciprocal theme' to produce the required reactions in the viewers. Various assumptions about the relationship between the psychological response and the physical stimuli are present in all these examples. In general they may be summarised as follows:

1.3.1. THAT THERE ARE CONSISTENT MECHANISMS RELATING PHYSICAL STIMULUS TO PSYCHOLOGICAL RESPONSE.—For instance, that blue rooms usually look bigger. The evidence for the existence of such relationships is examined in Chapter 3. But perhaps we can pre-empt ourselves a little by referring to the contextual problems and the possibility that such relationships may grow more out of the situation in which they are made (*e.g.* blue room after a yellow one) than the absolute stimuli themselves.

1.3.2. THAT THERE ARE NO CHANGES IN A PERSON'S RESPONSE TO THE SAME (OR SIMILAR) STIMULI OVER TIME.—As we have seen, amongst the many users of a building some will have very frequent contact with it, others will visit it very rarely. Thus some will have the opportunity to find their way about it and to discover ways of dealing with any intricacies in it, whilst others will be coming to it fresh with little opportunity for having learnt about it. Many buildings, however, seem to be designed as if the users come to them with a standard set of reactions which remain throughout their contact with the building. In Chapter 4 we shall look at the bases of the learning processes, and try to elucidate the conditions under which we might expect reactions to change.

1.3.3. THAT REACTIONS TO PHYSICAL STIMULI ARE INNATE.—It is a corollary of this assumption that we move through developmental stages as we mature, these stages being determined by our genetic make-up. The distinction between *development* and *learning* is thus a crucial theoretical one which helps to indicate which processes of change will be underlying themes from one age group to the next and which will be modifications wrought by the particular patterns of experience of any given individual. The type of practical question which closely relates to this assumption is, for instance, whether very different sorts of facilities should be provided for children of different ages in an institution such as a school or a children's hospital. These questions and the others which derive from them are explored in Chapter 5.

1.3.4. THAT PEOPLE ARE ESSENTIALLY SIMILAR IN THEIR INTER-ACTION WITH PHYSICAL STIMULI.—Because a great variety of people are associated with the production and use of most buildings, their design often proceeds as if everyone dealt with their physical surroundings in more or less the same way. Chapter 7 examines the patterns which psychologists have used to describe the differences found between people. The way in which this information may be applied practically has yet to be resolved, but, clearly, knowing something of the crucial dimensions along which people may differ would provide the framework for considering the range of design alternatives. If, for example, introversion were shown to be a critical dimension in relation to coping with the physical environment, but intelligence not, then providing buildings which allow for a range of differences in introversion would be more important than allowing for differences in intelligence.

In this discussion of individual differences we frequently come across the concept of an underlying dimension. This concept also plays an important role in many other areas of psychology and has thus developed an array of precise meanings and techniques associated with them. For that reason Chapter 6 is devoted to the concepts associated with underlying dimensions.

1.3.5. THAT PEOPLE DO NOT USE SPACE IN A RANDOM WAY.—This is one assumption for which we will find much support in psychology! But the question which follows is what processes can we discern which underlie the use of space. Are there, for instance, mechanisms inherited from our animal ancestors like 'territoriality'? Or do we use space more in keeping with our human capacity for abstract thinking? Chapter 8 explores these issues.

1.4. Organisations

As we have seen, few buildings, if any, are produced by one person on his own. Thus because of the necessity to communicate and organise, it is of considerable importance for the architect to know something about the psychological processes upon which organisations are based. The fact that many buildings are produced for large organisations increases the relevance of understanding these processes. Indeed it often surprises me that organisations of totally different structures are often housed in buildings of identical shape and form. Thus one of the points which emerges in Chapter 9, where we look at organisational psychology, is that consideration of the processes which facilitate the success of any particular organisation may often lead to much more appropriate environmental structures.

It is also in the context of organisations that we have the opportunity to examine briefly the motives which people have for remaining part of an organisation, in other words the aspects of their satisfaction at work. Perhaps it is a little paradoxical that such an important issue as motivation finds its way into the present book in the applied context of organisations. This, however, is quite intentional because it is in this context that it is of most importance to building designers. For instance, the question is often asked whether the physical surroundings at work, on which organisations often lavish money, really do contribute to worker satisfaction. Or whether, as is often argued, reactions to the physical surroundings are just representations of reactions to the organisation in general. Thus the evidence for these viewpoints could have a direct bearing upon the relative amounts it was worth spending upon different aspects of an organisation.

1.5. Psychological Information and Design

It might help to clarify further the potential psychological contribution to design by considering briefly three broad categories of psychological information which the designer requires and which would be better if supplied on the basis of psychological understanding.

1.5.1. ACTIVITY REQUIREMENTS.—What people do, where and when, and how these activities change (both over time and at different stages in life), provide some of the most fundamental information for design. Indeed, many designers begin by trying to list what these activities might be. However, simply knowing what these activities are (that people will eat and sleep in the building, for example) as if they were performed by a carefully programmed automaton, hides many of their important subtleties and makes it difficult to deal with irregularities or rapid changes (such as changes in eating habits over time). In order to cope with the complexities of human behaviour it is necessary to come to grips with the psychological mechanisms which give rise to it.

1.5.2. RELATIVE VALUES.—One of the central problems facing the architect is that of determining priorities. In any real world situation, resources of time, money, expertise or manpower are never infinite and so the range of possibilities for variation in any particular physical variable are limited. This means that the designers must determine the priorities and relative values of the various aspects of their design. They must for example decide whether to spend their money on better acoustic separation or better heating. To determine these priorities scientifically would demand the sort of profound understanding of behaviour which does not exist within psychology at the present time. Even with that understanding there would still be many moral and political issues to be resolved. However, steps in the direction of a scientific understanding of the psychological priorities involved must begin with an examination of the fundamentals of human behaviour.

1.5.3. BEHAVIOUR/ENVIRONMENT RELATIONSHIPS.—Often designers look to psychology for simple relationships between environmental and behavioural variables. They want to know what size of room would make people happy or perhaps more precisely the relationship between changes in, say, lighting level and productivity. They then feel that they could decide on the level they wanted or could afford and would read off the graph (so to speak) the implications of that decision. That the matter is not as simple as this might be expected. If the relationship were curved there would often be two possible levels, to give a more obvious complication. But because people *interact* with their environment rather than *react* to it, knowledge of simple relationships, without understanding the causes and correlates of those relationships, will not be sufficient for decision making.

1.6. The Contribution at Different Stages of Design

Like research, design does not take place at one moment in time and on the basis of one clearly defined set of decisions. As a consequence, the contribution of psychology will be different depending upon the stage at which the designer is. Three stages can be identified in design for each of which different types of psychological information are of most value.

1.6.1. CONCEPTION.—In the early stages the architect must clarify what it is the building is for, what is to go on within it and what the general objectives of the organisation it houses are. At this stage, therefore, the potential psychological contribution is equally general. The type of requirements the architect should consider can be clarified as can the general approaches which the architect should take towards the building. For instance, if psychological research indicates that certain aspects of a building will encourage specific types of behaviour (such as separate rooms leading to little informal contact between office workers) then it would suggest that the architect would be well advised to consider the possibilities for creating a building (a cellular office block, say) which contains those aspects at the appropriate levels. If, on the other hand, it was the way in which the users of the building were able to make sense of it or relate it to their own experiences which had emerged as a critical psychological factor (such as children thinking of a hospital as a type of 'school'), then this might suggest a totally different approach to the design (in terms, say, of its 'classroom-like' character rather than its 'adult-hospital' atmosphere).

1.6.2. SPECIFICATION.—Having clarified the main design requirements, the process of deciding upon the details of the design produced, sizes, shapes, relationships, services and so on gets under way. At this stage the architect looks to the psychologist for specific information which will relate physical variables to psychological ones. For instance, how brightness of colours might influence the wakefulness of the building users. Such categorical relationships of a broad general kind are unlikely to exist, but information relating to the specific problems (such as between loudness of a particular noise and performance on a particular task) may be found. The designers would, thus, at this stage receive further clarification of the critical factors to consider when detailing.

1.6.3. EVALUATION.—The third stage is to examine the existing building in order to learn from it what things should be repeated in the future and which mistakes to avoid. At this stage, the psychological contribution relates to orientating the designer to the aspects which he should evaluate. It is also a methodological one, providing him with techniques which could be used for measurement and evaluation.

The above stages have been discussed in relation to the design of a complete building, but it is possible to consider them existing both during the production of a building and after it has been inhabited. Whilst a building is being designed, conceptualisation, specification and evaluation may take place first by the production of sketch designs which give rise to detailed plans which are then specified in more detail and once more evaluated. Once the building is completed the users must grow to understand it to the degree that they can cope with and use detailed aspects of it, and in many cases, eventually evaluate that use and modify the building in the light of their evaluations.

With these various design cycles taking place and in view of the fact that they are analogous to the research process, it is possible to argue that architecture always has been, in some of its aspects, a branch of psychological research. It has just not been precisely organised enough to make it fit within the rubric of science. To my mind, one of the most fundamental weaknesses in this research aspect of architecture has been the absence of an awareness of the underlying psychological principles which may be drawn upon to develop it into a coherent aspect of science. Thus it is likely that understanding psychology and its processes *per se* will bring about an improvement in design decision making.

1.7. Conclusion

In such a brief book as this it will not be possible to cover all these issues in detail (or the many others there is no space to specify) but if I can stimulate architects to consider them and to look further for information the book will have served its purpose. If it also enables people to understand more readily the actual concepts and experiments they come across when looking further then its secondary purpose will have been fulfilled.

QUESTIONS FOR DISCUSSION

(1) What are the psychological assumptions underlying the design of a children's hospital, and an office block, how do they differ and what are the similarities?

(2) What groups of people are involved in the production of a prison? What difficulties of communication between them are likely to occur? Could the clarification of any psychological assumptions resolve these difficulties?

(3) In what ways could Le Corbusier's design for Ronchamp have benefited from psychological research?

(4) In what ways could the design of an airport terminal benefit from psychological research?

Chapter 2

Research

.

2.1. *A Study of Open-Plan Offices*

Before describing results it will be of value to illustrate the *process* of psychological research. So let us take as an example a study I carried out[1] which developed from the work of The Pilkington Research Unit.[2]

The research was initially specified as an attempt to find an optimum sized office space for clerical workers. This was considered to be an important problem because the configuration of modern city centres relates, in part, to the size of internal spaces provided within office buildings. Discussion with designers had shown that a major limitation is placed on the size of these internal spaces by the amount of daylight which it is decided to provide at the back of the rooms. However, Wells[3] had indicated that windows might possibly be of more importance in providing a view out than allowing daylight in. If this were the case then it would be possible to have very deep internal spaces, provided all the desks within any space had an unobstructed view out. This raises the subsequent problem of deciding upon the optimum size for these internal unobstructed spaces. Attitudinal studies[2] had shown that management preferred their clerical workers to be in quite large spaces but the clerical workers themselves preferred private ones. This conflict of attitudes could only be resolved by referring to the commercial context. It seemed possible that if the relationship between clerical performance and office size could be found then this could be weighed against administrative and psychological effects. A further motivation for looking for a relationship between office size and performance was that it would help test various theories of the nature of human performance and the things which affect it.

Because of the amount of background thought and information available it was thus possible to isolate a seemingly clear cut research project. I was simply to find the relationship between office size and clerical worker performance. The way to do this was to go to a number of offices of different sizes and give the workers a series of standard tasks to perform. Of course I would need to make sure that the workers I was testing in the different offices were similar to one another and that the results I was obtaining were due to the office environment and not some other irrelevant variable, such as their education, over which I had no control.

As a first stage in finding this relationship I needed to try out my measures of performance to find those which would give me the clearest relationships with office size. For this I went to one of the largest open offices in Europe and tested people in the open space as well as in private rooms for general use, which existed in the same building. Figures 2.1(a) and (b) illustrate the tests in progress in the two spaces.

Fig. 2.1(a).   Testing taking place in the open office.

Fig. 2.1(b).   Testing taking place in the private office.

If you have followed the argument so far, you will appreciate my dismay at finding that on the majority of measures there were no significant differences between performance in the two spaces. All thinking about the problem had revolved around the question of whether there was an increase or decrease in performance in rooms of different sizes. To find that no consistent differences could be detected between a room that held over a thousand people and a room that held two people suggested that the original conceptualisation of the problem was somehow deficient! At this stage it was therefore necessary to examine in more detail exactly what was this original conceptualisation. I thought I *had* worked out exactly what it was, but my inability to make sense of the results in any other way than saying that the environment was irrelevant for performance (at least for those aspects of environment and performance with which I had dealt) led me to the conclusion that there must have been some weakness in the way I had done this. I could not accept that the physical environment was irrelevant because so many people thought it was relevant and also because there had been many laboratory studies which had shown a direct effect of environmental variables on performance on tasks similar to those I had used.[4]

Re-thinking led me to the conclusion that my original view of the relationship between environment and performance had been too static and simple. I had assumed that the distractions of a large space would have a direct effect on the responses people produced, because there were simple and straightforward limits to people's capabilities that could be exceeded or overloaded in a direct way by variables in the physical surroundings. It became apparent that in order to deal adequately with my results it was necessary to draw upon a more complex model of behaviour. For instance it now seemed useful to consider the possibility that motivation or interest could enable people to get over distractions from their surroundings, or that the sort of people who took jobs in open offices were those upon whom the environment had little effect. A further possibility was that my measuring instruments were not sensitive enough to reveal any differences. The question which follows from this possibility is that if a wide variety of measurements made over a forty minute period cannot show any effect what type of effect are we looking for? Is it likely to be an important effect considering the context of the problem?

The lack of any clear relationship between room size and performance thus led to a whole series of new possibilities which needed to be tested. A new set of measurements was therefore made in other offices and it was found (when dealing with room sizes within the range of five people to one hundred people) that some relationship could be found between the general ability of the clerical workers and the room in which they work. This relationship is such that workers of less ability tend to be found in larger rooms (even when the rooms of different sizes were in the same department and the occupants were of a similar status doing similar work) and thus indicated that there might well be some process of selection, or self-selection, which tended to lead to different sorts of people working in different rooms. Time and money ran out before this further assumption of a selection process could be examined and tested in detail.

2.2. *The Nature of Scientific Research*

The above description of a research project is rather unusual. It is unusual because it is frank about the mistakes and inefficiencies involved, and because it describes (albeit briefly), as accurately as is possible a number of years after the event, the sequence of thought processes through which the research worker went. Just as the architect has some ideas which he wants to try out, so the research worker has a number of assumptions which he is trying to test. Both of them have limited resources of time and money and must work within the abilities they have or the expertise they can draw upon. Contrary to the belief held in some quarters, research scientists are mere mortals who make mistakes and run up overdrafts, just like architects, or anybody else.

This point has to be emphasised because for many reasons research is reported as if this were not the case. It is reported in a finished, digested form according to a standard format. The most important reason for this is the public nature of research, the need for *objectivity*.

The strength of science lies in the fact that results are built upon one another. This is only possible because each investigator produces his results together with information that will enable others to decide for themselves whether to agree or disagree with his conclusions, or indeed enable them to see if they can obtain further supporting evidence.

The linkage of relationship which grows from this approach can be seen in the office size example. It was necessary to accept previous findings on daylight or on the effects of distractions on performance in laboratory experiments, in order to proceed with the formulation of the research problem to be studied. It would not have been possible to build with confidence on these earlier findings if there had not been some general agreement about them. This agreement can only be based upon two things. First, that the logic by which the conclusions are drawn is sound, and secondly, that they are founded upon empirical evidence. The need to use measurement as an integral part of the scientific process relates very closely to the need for publicly attestable objectivity. If people cannot agree about the evidence, about whether it actually exists or not, then there is little likelihood of them being able to agree with anything derived from this evidence. Personal experience no matter how intense for the individual is not open to scrutiny by others (unless it is expressed in some form such as words). Data which are collected in an agreed way, such that two people working independently could collect the same data, is the only possible basis for any process of human reasoning which is to be truly cumulative.

2.3. Aspects of Objectivity

Because of the central role of objectivity in scientific investigations much effort has been put into finding the best ways of achieving this. This effort has centred around two aspects of the scientific process; first, measurement and, secondly, the efficient control of all the relevant variables.

2.3.1. MEASUREMENT.—As the measurement of observable phenomena is the only type of evidence on which scientific judgements can be based, considerable attention has been given to ways of making measurements and of testing that the measurements are not influenced by irrelevant factors. Two properties of measurement that must be present to a high degree, if the measurement is to be of any value, have been isolated; *reliability* and *validity*.

The reliability of a measuring instrument is the degree to which it will give the same measurements under identical conditions on two separate occasions; in more technical terms, the size of its correlation with itself. If a measurement does not correlate highly with itself on two separate occasions it cannot be expected to correlate highly with any other variables. For this reason all psychological measurements, whether they be measures of attitude, intelligence, personality, performance or any other aspect of behaviour, are tested in a number of ways before they are used to ensure that they have a reasonable reliability. These tests can be carried out in many different ways but the most common are:

(1) by collecting data from the same people under similar conditions on two separate occasions; *e.g.* an intelligence test would be given to the same school children on two occasions a week

apart and the correlation between the scores of the children on the two occasions would be a measure of the 'test-re-test' reliability of that particular measure of intelligence;

(2) the relation between two different forms of the instrument which were ostensibly measuring the same thing gives an indication of the 'parallel forms reliability';

(3) the relation between two halves of the same test gives an indication of the 'split half', or 'internal reliability'.

The validity of a measuring instrument is best thought of as an indication of the degree to which it measures what it is thought to measure. Reliability can be seen as one aspect of this because a measure of intelligence which is more sensitive to differences in the weather than differences in school children is likely to produce quite different scores on two different occasions. It could then be thought of as a useful measure of intelligence only if intelligence is defined as some psychological response to the weather! But it is apparent that in this unlikely situation it would still be necessary to show that the test actually does correlate with other measures of the meteorological situation. As Campbell and Fiske[5] have argued, all validity consists of two components: a convergent one, which is the degree to which the measurement relates to other measures to which it would be expected to relate, and a discriminant component, which is the degree to which it does not relate to other measures to which it would not be expected to relate.

How do we 'expect' something of a measuring instrument? Our expectations lie in the theory or assumptions from which the decision to carry out the measurements was derived. In other words, estimates of the validity of a measurement are based on similar processes to those touched on at the beginning of our discussion of scientific research. Assumptions are made which are tested empirically. For instance, the assumption that a set of items measures, say, general satisfaction may be tested by showing that scores on those items relate to other accepted criteria of satisfaction. This is inevitably a cyclical process; first an assumption of what a measure measures is made, then this assumption is tested. The measure is then modified in the light of the test and tested again and so on until eventually some consistent description of what the test is actually measuring emerges. Thus instruments which were initially thought of as tests of ability have ended up as measures of personality (*e.g.* Reference 6) and some general knowledge questionnaires have been shown to be useful for measuring attitudes.[7]

Not all measuring instruments have all the properties they ought to have. They may be reliable but it may be difficult to know what they are measuring. What they are measuring may be agreed upon but not the actual numbers which should be put on the responses. A further complication arises from the fact that the validity of a highly reliable measurement may be questioned because people are responding to being measured rather than simply responding. However, the history of psychology has shown that progress can be made without a 'perfect' measuring instrument and has in fact developed a wide range of extremely valuable ways of measuring behaviour. It is worth while considering the range available in order to see the actual measurements discussed in later chapters in perspective. The best way of covering this range is from the viewpoint of the dimensions along which measurements may be considered.

(1) Open–closed: the range and type of responses which the respondent may produce or which are recorded may be very limited or may be very wide indeed. For instance, the number of eye blinks per minute might be counted or we might record a group discussion and put the comments made into broad categories. The more open the measurement the less objective and hence reliable is it likely to be, although this is not an inevitable relationship.

(2) Verbal–physiological: the range of possible responses to stimuli is sometimes usefully thought of as running along a dimension from the spoken word to physiological reactions such as heartbeat. The middle of this range may be thought of as controlled performance tasks or sensory-motor responses such as speed of reaction to a buzzer. It is possible to get highly reliable measurements at any point along this dimension.

(3) Reactive–non-reactive: the measurements made may vary from those in which the subject's reaction to being measured has a great influence, to those in which he does not react at all. For instance, in a personal interview concerning the frequency of

imbibing alcoholic drinks the subject may hide his true behaviour because of the opinions he thinks the interviewer holds. If the same interviewer were to count the number of wine bottles and beer cans in the respondent's dustbin then that measurement would not be sensitive to the respondent's opinions about being measured (although he might well react to the measurement process itself his reaction would not influence the measurements made unless on subsequent occasions he started burying the evidence).

(4) Overt–covert: although the respondent may react to the act of measurement it is still possible that what the investigator is interested in is different from what the respondent thinks. For instance, on the one hand the investigator may ask for stories to be produced describing the activities in a particular picture and indicate that it is a measure of creativity, whereas what the investigator is really interested in is the emotional problems revealed through the stories. On the other hand, a public opinion poll does little more than ask people for their opinion.

The particular instrument which it is decided to use depends both upon the theoretical considerations which give rise to the need for measurement and to the practical possibilities. If the theory takes into account the fact that people are also responding to being measured (as is the case with public opinion research) then an obtrusive reactive measurement can be validly used. If the theory assumes that the psychological process being studied is below a person's level of awareness then there is little value in trying to study that process by direct verbal means. It is also the case that different types of measurement will be of value at different stages in a research project. For instance, when problems are still not clearly formulated an open ended approach will probably be the most fruitful. It must be emphasised that no one method of measurement is the best one for all purposes. Furthermore, the greater the variety of measurements which can be shown to produce relationships which support the initial assumptions, the more valid are those assumptions. This is the case because each method of measurement will have different biases and thus overall the biases of the different methods should counteract one another. It was in view of this that a range of measurements of performance were made in the study of office size, including such measures as simple clerical checking tasks and simulated telephone answering.

2.3.2. CONTROL.—As we have seen, one development from the need for objectivity in science is the growth of a great range of methods of measurement. The second is the use of a variety of methods for *controlling* the variables of relevance in any particular project. This enables the researcher to establish the nature of the links between the phenomena being measured in such a way that common agreement upon those links is possible.

There are essentially two types of approach to the problem of control encountered in science, one in which the *relationships* between a series of variables are examined and the other, in which it is *differences* between situations at which the scientist looks. Both these types of inquiry require that variables extraneous to those being studied do not have any influence that would invalidate the conclusions drawn from the study.

Thus, for instance, in the study of open offices it was necessary to ensure that all the respondents had similar skills and were the same age and sex. This reduced the possibility that differences in performance were due to these other variables rather than room size.

It will be seen that a critical word is 'cause'. If we are interested in causal relationships then we must make sure that account has been taken of all the other plausible causes as well as the one we are checking. If, however, we only want to predict one thing from another then our controls need not be so stringent. In fact from research into relationships (which usually take the form of surveys) it is extremely difficult to draw conclusions about causality. To do this studies of differences are necessary. Taking again the office example, in the second stage a series of measurements of performance in different sized rooms were made. However, in order to examine some of the causes of the relationships found between room size and performance it was necessary to see if there were any differences between groups who normally worked in the office and those who were introduced into it for the purposes of the experiment.

The laboratory experiment is the classical example of studies of differences aimed at establishing causal relationships. A variable of interest (the independent variable) is produced at different levels, through the introduction of changes by the experimenter, and the concomitant differences found in the other variables being measured (the dependent variables) are recorded. In the first stage of the study of office size the two rooms provided the two levels of independent variable (room size) and the various measures of performance were the dependent variables. It is precisely because the experimenter has control over the levels of the independent variable and can assign subjects to the conditions in which they occur that he can argue that any difference found in the dependent variables is *caused* by variations in the levels of the independent variables.

Unfortunately, this type of classical laboratory experiment is very time consuming and inefficient because only one set of independent variables can be examined at any one time. The experimental

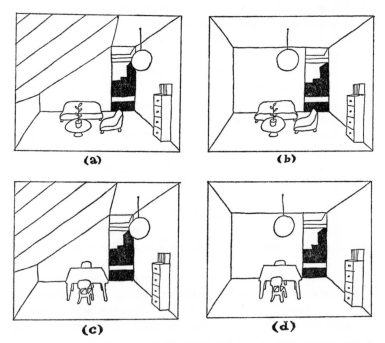

Fig. 2.2.   An example of rooms designed experimentally to allow causal links to be established.

approach has therefore been developed to allow the experimenter to examine the effects of more than one variable at a time. A further advantage of this is that the effects produced by interactions between the variables can also be identified. Figure 2.2 shows an example of this taken from studies of people's assessment of the friendliness of interiors.[8] It will be seen that in Figure 2.2, parts (a) and (c) differ from (b) and (d) only in terms of the angle of the roof. Thus if we ask people to evaluate each of these rooms on a series of rating scales we can look at the difference between the average ratings of the two groups of drawings and thus see the effect of roof angle. On the other hand, we can compare the differences between the average

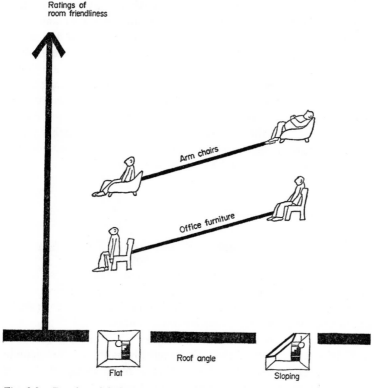

Fig. 2.3. Results of judgements of drawings similar to those illustrated in Figure 2.2.

response to (a) and (b) and the average response to (c) and (d) in order to find the effects of furniture arrangement. The overall pattern of responses, shown for instance by whether the *difference* between (a) and (b) is any larger or smaller than the *difference* between (c) and (d), will indicate whether there is any interaction between roof angle and furniture arrangement in the effects they produce. The actual results from the ratings of architecture undergraduates of drawings like these on friendliness can be seen in Figure 2.3. There it can be seen that the rooms with the easy chairs are rated as more friendly and that although a sloping roof has a similar effect it is not so great. The fact that the lines are parallel suggests that there is no interaction between these variables.

This approach to the presentation of stimuli or the organisation of levels of the independent variables (in this case, roof angle and furniture arrangements) is usually referred to as factorial design and the statistical process for analysing the data is usually the analysis of variance. Both factorial design and analysis of variance are simple examples of the large area of statistics known as multi-variate statistics. This allows the examination of the effects of and relationships between a great range of variables in one investigation. Factor analysis which we will be looking at in Chapter 6 is another multivariate statistical technique, but one which concentrates on the relationships between variables rather than the differences.

2.4. The Study of Variance

We have already touched on the fact that scientific investigations may help to predict one thing from another, or more generally establish the relationship between two phenomena, or that on the other hand they may show how one variable leads to or causes another. All these different types of scientific finding help to contribute to understanding the variables being studied.

It may have been noted that words like 'variable', 'variance' and 'variate' have occurred frequently in our discussion of the scientific approach. The reason for this is that a more technical way of describing these processes is as an attempt to understand and explain variation.

The most usual statistical measure of this is the measure of *variance* and I will restrict the discussion here to concepts related to that. All the things psychologists study vary. People differ in a variety of ways, the behaviour they produce and the things they respond to differ also. It is because of the awareness we all have of this wide range of differences that some have suggested that the scientific study of people is not possible. However, by trying to explain these observable variations and to find principles underlying them psychologists are putting this suggestion to the test. Every time a psychologist shows that there is a relationship between the variation found in one variable and the variation found in another, he is refuting the suggestion that people are too wildly different and random in what they do to allow of scientific study.

All statistics are really ways of summarising observable variability. Correlations, for instance, are measures of the degree to which variations within two variables correspond and the analysis of variance is a technique for showing that the differences in variance of the same measurement in two conditions (*e.g.* the difference between the variance of 'friendliness' ratings between sloping and flat roofs) is greater than the unexplained or error variance.

However, scientific psychology is more than just the statistical manipulation of variability. For this manipulation to be of value it must be expressed in terms general enough to suggest further possibilities. Thus, the general suggestion that distractions reduce performance leads to the possibility that office workers will not perform so well in big offices because of greater distractions there. Underlying the assumption that distractions may reduce performance is a set of ideas that help to explain it. There may be a number of different explanations. One might be that people are limited in their capabilities and that distractions overload these to the degree that performance is reduced. Another might be that people do not like distractions and show this dislike by performing less well. Both of these explanations are the rough outlines of theories about particular aspects of behaviour.

The important thing about scientific theories is that they give rise to the possibility of producing findings which will test those theories. If these possibilities are formulated precisely enough to enable the scientist to specify the results to expect in controlled studies of variance, then they may be called hypotheses. The test of an hypothesis (whether or not the results follow expectations) is thus inevitably the test of the theory from which it came and consequently of the assumptions on which the theory was based. The process of science can therefore be thought of as a sequence running; assumptions-theory-hypotheses-data-hypotheses-theory, etc. In actual practice this sequence is broken into at almost any point and an examination of the example given at the beginning of the chapter will show the sort of mixtures of sequence which are possible. However, the most logical sequence starts with assumptions and finishes with data. In order to further the objective nature of science the more obvious and logical the sequence described the easier it is for other scientists to make use of that piece of research. This is the reason why research proceeds in one way and is described in another. Another way of putting this is that description of research is an important stage in the scientific process and has its own rules like every other stage.

2.5. Values

A final reference in this chapter should be made to scientific values. Some architects fear that the last vestige of humanity and culture which they defend is now under attack from psychologists. They fear that given their chance psychologists will strike the death blow to artistic freedom and creativity. There are a number of factors which should help to allay these fears. First, an examination of the history of psychology shows that it has always given more to the arts than it has taken away, whether it be the effect of psychoanalytic theories on the surrealists or the contribution of perceptual psychology to 'Op art'. Secondly, it is becoming increasingly apparent from the development of psychological theories that originality, novelty or creativity are an important part of the psychological processes and as such can only be encouraged by study.

The final reason derives from a curious paradox in the scientific process. We have discussed in some detail in this chapter the objective, empirical methods available to the scientist for resolving research problems. We have said almost nothing about where these research problems come from. Some of the reasons for selecting any particular problem will be practical, some will relate to things suggested by other research but by far the most important reasons will be the scientist's own interests and values. Once architects have some understanding of psychology they will be in a strong position to specify research problems and thus to ensure that their values also influence the course of psychological research.

QUESTIONS FOR DISCUSSION

Below is a list of questions similar to those sometimes asked by architects of psychologists. How would *you* go about carrying out research (or redefining the questions) to answer them?

(1) Do pleasant surroundings make people work better?
(2) Do people really need daylight?
(3) What is it more important to spend money on in a building; acoustic separation or lighting?
(4) Is the Sydney Opera House a good building?
(5) Which rooms should be nearest a headmaster's in a school?
(6) What level of illumination is best for typing?
(7) Is there a relationship between education and aesthetic appreciation?

(In dealing with these questions the following should be borne in mind:

(a) The question posed may not be the exact *research* question which can be studied.
(b) It is necessary to decide what needs to be *measured* and what *controlled*.
(c) The form of the *analysis* and the method of *interpreting* the results are a crucial part of any research programme.)

Chapter 3

Perceptual Judgements

3.1. Context Effects

If you were to put into one bowl some cold water, into a second bowl some warmish water and into a third bowl some hot water, you would have the apparatus for the interesting experiment John Locke described in 1690. First you place your right forefinger into the hot water and your left forefinger into the cold water and leave them there for a minute or two. You then take both fingers out, shake them for a second or two to get the drips off and insert them both together into the lukewarm water. What you will then experience is an effect that seems to run through all perceptual activity. This is an elementary contrast effect. The previous experience has somehow changed your perceptions. The contrast with the hot water makes the lukewarm water feel cold to the right forefinger. The contrast with the cold water makes the lukewarm water feel hot to the left forefinger.

The contrast effect in relation to touch is part of common experience. However, it comes as a surprise to many people (although Beebe-Center[1] demonstrated the effect very many years ago) that the same sort of thing can be demonstrated with judgements which are not so directly related to the function of the sense organs, for instance to judgements of visual pleasantness. Some of our students recently made ratings of a number of photographs of houses existing in and around Glasgow (by giving them a mark out of 10 for 'pleasantness'). First, each of fifty people rated all the photographs, each individual seeing them in a different order. From this first rating three sets of photographs were selected. The first group of photographs was composed of those which were rated highly, the second of those with low ratings and the third of those rated average on general pleasantness. A second series of judgements was now made by another group of students. In this series some of the neutral photographs were rated after the 'pleasant' photographs and the others after the 'unpleasant' ones. The scores for this second set of judgements are given in Table 3.1. There it can be seen that the ratings for the neutral houses after the unfavourable houses are all higher than after the favourable houses. This shows a clear effect of the context upon the ratings of even so seemingly abstract a judgement as pleasantness.

Table 3.1

Mean ratings of pleasantness of houses in different contexts

Photograph no.	After 'pleasant' houses	After 'unpleasant' houses
1	4·0	5·3
2	4·8	6·7
3	3·3	5·7
4	2·7	4·5
5	5·5	6·9
6	2·2	4·8

Our social situation can also be shown to act as another type of context which influences, to a marked degree, the way we perceive. An experiment by Sherif[2] shows this quite clearly. In this experiment he used the phenomenon known as the autokinetic effect produced by the observation of a point of light in a darkened room. Although the experimenter keeps the light quite still, after a time subjects get the impression that it is moving. The amount and type of this movement is related to many things but if responses are made in a group context the individual's response (and don't forget this is an indication of what he says he actually sees) slowly fits in with the group norm. Figure 3.1 shows a schematic representation of the amount of movement which might be seen by two individuals first when they make judgements on their own and subsequently when they make judgements in three sessions as members of the same group.

There have been many similar studies (*e.g.* Reference 3) all of which support the common experience that the way we see things differs according to the social situation in which we see them. It is even suggested at times (Gombrich, Reference 4) that the social contribution of art is to modify the way in which we look at the world about us, just as the world about us modifies the way we look at art.

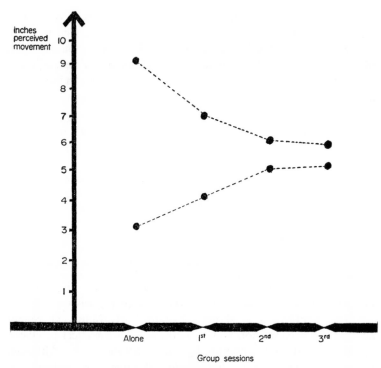

Fig. 3.1. An illustration of the effect of group membership on amount of perceived autokinetic movement.

One important implication follows from the existence of these contextual effects. This is that sensations (*i.e.* that which impinges on the sense organs) cannot really be studied by psychologists independently of the perceptions, cognitions and other aspects of human experience which are associated with them. In other words, it makes little psychological sense to talk about the 'sharp eye', the 'sensitive ear' or about the environment 'playing tricks' with our *senses*, although some psychologists sometimes fall into language habits which ignore this. These descriptions can be shown to be inaccurate because no sense organ could be influenced by a group of people. We deal with the world then, for the most part, as conscious integrated human beings, not as responding eyes, ears, hands or for that matter, brains.

3.2. The Gestalt Laws

The complexity which has been described above does not mean that general perceptual principles cannot be found, but that the principles which are found will relate more closely to relative judgements or context effects rather than to absolute levels. It does mean that any principles which are established may not be given the role of natural and inevitable laws. They are better considered as guidelines of varying values, depending on the contexts in which attempts may be made to apply them.

Whilst the founders of this school would give greater universality to their formulations than many other psychologists, there is little doubt that one such set of principles has been produced by the Gestalt school of psychologists.[5] The principles which they put

Fig. 3.2(a).   An illustration of 'figure/ground'.

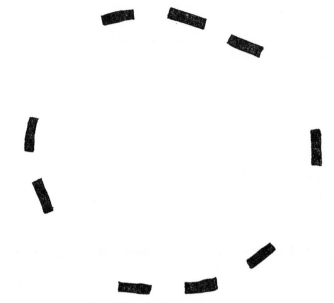

Fig. 3.2(b).   An illustration of 'closure'.

forward make an important contribution to our understanding of perception.

One of their central concepts was *prägnanz*. This means literally something akin to 'goodness'. The idea behind it is that any configuration is perceived in such a way as to make it appear as simple, clear or comprehensible as possible. This aspect of perception has been studied in the main with reference to simple line drawings of an abstract nature. Thus in Figure 3.2(a) we have a shaded shape lying in an unshaded square. Only in the most unusual circumstances can this be perceived as two inter-related abstract shapes. We are forced to see the shaded shape as some unidentifiable object lying on top of a white square. Indeed it is difficult to describe Figure 3.2(a) without referring to the shaded part as if it were a *figure* and the unshaded square as a *ground*.

Gestalt psychologists regarded this tendency to see objects in terms of figures on a ground as a prerequisite necessary before the principles of *prägnanz* could come into operation. From the general

Fig. 3.2(c). Proximity and similarity as forces in perceptual structuring.

viewpoint of perception leading to the simplification and stabilisation of the stimuli presented to the brain, it is clear that the figure and ground phenomenon plays an important role in helping us to structure the world we see. The principles of *prägnanz* have a similar role.

There are a number of ways in which we give objects *prägnanz*. They can be most easily described by specifying the properties we try to superimpose upon any configuration with which we are presented. These properties include those of symmetry, regularity and continuity. Configurations which do not have these properties will be perceived, or at least remembered, as if they do. For example, Figure 3.2(b) will be thought of as a circle although the circle is incomplete and if it were to be completed it may have many irregularities. Where the configuration cannot readily be seen as one figure, there is a tendency to group it perceptually on the basis of such things as proximity or similarity. So that, for instance, Figure 3.2(c) is not perceived as a totally random array of dots and dashes but rather as groups, the similar stimuli being grouped together or the stimuli close together being perceptually grouped together.

Initially there was an attempt by some Gestalt psychologists to explain the various phenomena in physiological terms.[6] However, these explanations have proved for the most part to be untenable, because of the evidence showing the lack of complete generality of these phenomena and the changes in them with development through childhood (Vernon, 1970). Furthermore, people with an architectural background will realise the weakness of drawing generalisations from experiments based on such a limited range of stimuli. It will be apparent to them that these studies rely heavily upon the processes of representation and the information we have learnt to read from line drawings.

However, the Gestalt studies are a further illustration of the point made earlier. Namely, that perception is not based upon isolated responses to particular stimuli, but rather as a reaction to the total stimulus field. The essence of Gestalt psychology is often summarised as the whole being greater than the sum of its parts. Another implication of this is that perception is an active reaction to the world about us not a passive response. We actively structure and make sense of the stimuli with which we are presented.

3.3. *Stevens's Power Law*

There are, of course, many perceptual phenomena which require some assumptions to be made about what is happening at the sense organs, in other words, which are particular reactions to sensations. But as we shall see even these require interpretations beyond simple physiological explanation. Stevens has shown on a number of occasions[7] that psychological judgements relate to one another and to the physical phenomena they are judgements of on the basis of the ratios between them. In other words judgements of the relative brightness of two light sources can usually be made very accurately indeed, whereas judgements of the absolute brightness are often erroneous. One consequence of this is that, as the physical stimulus increases in quantity, relatively larger changes in it are necessary for those changes to be perceptually distinguishable. The mathematical result of this is that the logarithm of any physical stimulus is directly and simply related to the logarithm of the psychological magnitude estimated. Another way of putting this is to say that the psychological judgement (p) is a power function of the magnitude of the physical stimulus (s):

$$p = s^\alpha$$

(where α changes according to the physical variables under examination). This is known as Stevens's Power Law.

Of particular importance in helping us to understand the broader implications of the power law are the further studies carried out by Stevens and his colleagues[8] using non-physical stimuli. For instance, he has shown that with criminals the sentence given and the judged severity of the crime are related to each other by a power function. The fact that this relationship can be shown to exist across such a broad range of judgements lends support to the general arguments of this chapter; first that perceptual judgements cannot be isolated from other types of psychological judgements and, secondly, that it is the relative relationship between stimuli which is of central importance in determining judgements.

3.4. *Perceptual Constancy and the Perception of Space*

There is one perceptual phenomenon which has always interested psychologists but which laymen often have difficulty in thinking of

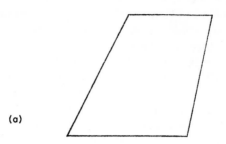

(a)

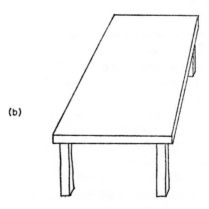

(b)

Fig. 3.3.   Perceptual constancy.

as a 'phenomenon' at all. This is perceptual constancy. To many people it comes as a surprise that the sensations they receive from the world about them are very varied although their perceptions are relatively stable. For instance, a wall painted white is unlikely to be physically the same colour along its full length, especially if a bright light is shining on it, but we perceive it or think of it as a white wall in all but exceptional circumstances. Similarly, because the retina is essentially two dimensional, a square table will give rise to an image on the retina which is only rarely square. It will vary from diamond to trapezoid depending on our angle of view. Indeed the use of perspective drawing relates to this, but nonetheless we usually *perceive* the table as a square one. We must *learn* how to draw in perspective. Figures 3.3(a) and (b) illustrate the way in which our perceptions of actual forms maintain constancy. Both the polygons are the same shape but the one which is seen as representing a table will be perceived as rectangular.

Besides shape and brightness constancy, we experience colour and size constancy in much the same way. Perceptual constancies are thus an excellent example of the way in which our knowledge of the world modifies what we perceive. If we 'know' what an object is, we know and perceive it as the appropriate size, shape, etc. It is a task, requiring some training, to isolate the abstract formal qualities of the object. Thus to an architect a brick may be seen as an interesting pattern of pink and red textures, but to the average layman it is seen as a brick, 'the sort of thing from which buildings are made'. Furthermore, the constancies of perception, be they size, hue, brightness or any other perceptual dimension, can only be broken down under the sort of unusual circumstances that can be created in a psychological laboratory. The essence of these circumstances, as illustrated by Ames[9] for instance, is that the context of the object being perceived is removed or distorted so that cues normally available for distinguishing the attribute in question, say size, are absent or so presented as to give a misleading impression. For instance, in Figure 3.4 an experiment[10] using playing cards is illustrated. These are normally assumed to be a similar size, but for the experiment they are in fact of different sizes. They are presented, however, so that the cues to distance such as texture which normally help us to ascertain the size of objects we know are absent. This leads to the distorted perception of the actual distances and sizes involved as illustrated. The important point about this experiment is that it illustrates that it is our knowledge of what the world is like, built up from previous experience, which creates these distortions of perception.

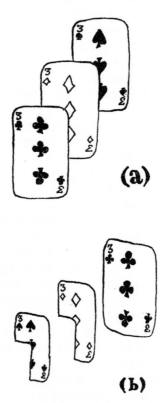

Fig. 3.4. An experiment on depth perception (a) Display as perceived; (b) actual set-up.

A simple architectural example of this may help to clarify its implications. Figure 3.5 is based upon the internal elevations of one of the walls of the Students' Union dining room at Liverpool University. The peculiarity of this room relates to our previous knowledge, and hence present expectations, of doors, windows and light fittings, their size in relation to one another and to the building as a whole. Clearly by playing upon these expectations or going along with them the architect can produce a great range of effects, from the commonplace to the unacceptable.

Fig. 3.5.   An example of conflicts of scale in buildings.

In general terms, the same can be said of the perception of space. In so far as it is understood by present day psychologists, it seems that the perception of space is based, in the main, upon the use of cues that are normally associated with distance in our daily life. These cues are the sorts of things which artists use, such as parallax, the difference in gradients of texture with different distances and the apparent convergence of parallel lines. Clearly many of these cues are learnt, together with the possibly subtler cues from bodily sensations such as convergence of the eyes for focusing and the relationships between what we can see and what we can feel with our hands. How early they are learnt and whether there is any innate component is open to discussion but as we shall see in Chapter 5 there is some evidence to suggest that our perception of space develops very early in life.

By way of summarising let me point to the dilemma in which early scientific psychologists found themselves. The eye receives a variety of stimuli from the same objects and all of these occur upon an essentially two-dimensional retina, however, the world we perceive is manifestly stable and three-dimensional; a square table is seen as such no matter what variety of two-dimensional configurations from it are presented to the retina. These psychologists asked how such a strange phenomenon could be possible. My argument has been that it is their viewpoint which was strange for it is not a retina which perceives but a person. People have a wide range of previous experience to draw upon and thus perception relies upon a variety of sources other than the retina, not least of which is the experience stored in the brain.

In relation to architecture, at a general level, as Ittelson[11] has pointed out there is much to suggest that there are environmental constancies much as there are the types of object constancies we have been discussing. Thus a church will be thought of as such, even though it has been converted for use as a warehouse. Similarly the repeated findings discussed in many of the references listed in the Appendix that various forms of environmental simulation (such as slides or models) produce closely comparable results, may be explained as an example of the perceptual constancy of the places depicted. For instance, take the study by Nagase,[12] in which photographs of famous buildings taken at set distances from the buildings, were shown to produce identical responses no matter what the distance. In this case it seems likely that people were giving their rating of the buildings *per se*, their concepts of them (just like our concept of the square table) built up over some time. They were not responding in a simple direct way to the stimuli impinging on their retinas.

3.5. Attention

One recurrent theme in our discussion of perceptual judgements has been the importance of context, the situation, or set of perceptual stimuli, within which the stimulus in question is perceived. However, it follows that a distinction between the stimulus and its context is essential to perception. In other words, perception is only possible because we *attend* to various aspects of our environment. We are not aware of all of it at any given point of time but can only become aware of a proportion of it by selectively attending to different aspects.

From the earliest days of psychology it has been clear that a person's attention span is severely limited usually to only about six discrete entities. This span can be shown in a number of ways, for instance, as the number of random digits which can be remembered over a short period of time[13] or the number of objects that can be accurately identified when presented briefly.[14] One consequence of this is that attention itself plays an important role in perception and needs to be taken account of when considering the design of actual environments.

One example of the implication of the phenomenon of selective attention for design is the psychological effect of formal plans of buildings. Designers sometimes act as if the bird's-eye view they have of a building from its plan is somehow transmitted to the users, and hence there is a need to make that plan look as neat and formal as possible. The mere fact of attention suggests that this is a spurious exercise as no user of the building can ever be aware at a given moment in time of all the aspects which make up the plan. At a more specific level, any designer using a coding system for identifying parts of his building or routes within it, which had more than six or seven elements should not be surprised if many of his building users are confused on their first attempts to use the code.

A further important aspect of attention is shown by Broadbent[15] in his discussion of the studies which have shown that it is easier to attend to some aspects of a stimulus than to others. For instance, differences in the sex of speakers is easier for people to attend to than many aspects of what they say.

3.6. Arousal

Of possibly wider architectural implication is the growing body of research concerned with the effects of the general environmental context in providing stimulation. The broad effect being such that aspects of behaviour such as the ability to attend, or general performance in response to stimuli, seem to be related to optimal levels of general environmental stimulation.

However, it must be emphasised that these ideas grew out of studies of extreme environmental conditions, far removed from the day to day experience of even the most monotonous street scene. Thus attempts to relate these ideas directly to the design of the built environment have to be treated with great caution.

The early studies in this area (Hebb[16]) were carried out in sensory deprivation experiments. In these experiments all forms of sensation a person might receive were removed or kept as constant as possible. For instance, in one series of experiments the subjects laid on a bed in a dark room wearing earphones playing a hissing noise with their arms and legs covered in sheaths so that they received no sensations from moving them.[17] It was found that besides the fact that people could only tolerate these conditions for a few hours one of the most marked effects was the reduction in their ability to concentrate or attend to specific stimuli. The presence or absence of the 'panic button' (to be used when the subject could not tolerate the situation any longer) also had a marked effect on how long he remained voluntarily. From the viewpoint of psychology the relevance of these studies, and the many others since carried out[18] is the indication that there may be an optimum level of stimulation for efficient performance. This appears to relate to the effect of stimulation on perceptual organisation. Furthermore, some studies have indicated that there is a part of the brain specifically responsible for modifying and organising perception which is itself enervated by the general level of stimulation in the environment.[17] Many theories have grown out of this postulated mechanism and include such things as an explanation of differences between people which is discussed in Chapter 7,[18] a theory for the origins of schizophrenia[19] and, possibly of most importance for architecture, an account of the basis of aesthetic experience.[20]

3.7. Some Broader Considerations

Having given briefly the broad outline of perceptual phenomena as examined by psychologists, we are in a position to look at some of the broader 'aesthetic' questions which architects frequently look to the psychology of perception to answer.

The first question is the one which searches for rules, often of proportions, in perception which determine what form or combination of forms will be 'beautiful'. For instance, the 'golden mean' is the relationship which is often given as an example of the rule which works and the request is then made for all the other rules. It should now be apparent that the approach outlined so far in this chapter would lead to being sceptical of any such all-embracing 'rules'. Valentine,[21] who examined the experimental research into many problems in aesthetics, showed that the golden mean does not inevitably produce a satisfying configuration. Edge[22] went further and showed that a building drawn according to the modular of Le Corbusier was no more likely to be rated as good than one looking like a Le Corbusier building but having different proportions. The explanations for these negative findings can be found in our earlier discussion. If perception is related to the context and previous experience of the observer, then it is unlikely that any abstract relationship, which does not take account of the context and the personal factors which a person brings to his judgements, will prove valid in a wide range of situations.

What is true of the golden mean is true also of the rules which have attempted to relate colours and emotion. Here again we cannot expect a given colour to produce a given response in all situations. Besides the perceptual phenomena of constancy and contrast which will modify the purely physical effects, the other more personal variables relating in particular to previous experience and the situation in which the colour is encountered will have a large influence. Clearly there will be a difference in emotional reaction to a red bus as opposed to a red breast and there is no reason to suppose that in many other examples there will be more convergence of response.

Another area in which it is often assumed that there are clear psychological relationships is between colour and perceived size or distance. Considering how widely held are the beliefs amongst designers that, say, blue makes things seem farther away and red makes them seem nearer, it is surprising how little real research has been carried out. However, that[23] which has been carried out, has produced the indeterminant results which we might expect.

There is, however, one area in which relationships of the sort designers hope for have been found. This is between colour names (or concepts) and emotional reactions (or preferences). The difference between asking people whether they like 'red' or whether it makes things seem larger, and actually showing people a red object and asking them whether they like its red colour or to estimate how large it is, is a major difference. In the former case we are dealing essentially with attitudes and beliefs whereas in the latter we are dealing with perceptions. Of course, as has been stressed throughout this chapter, the distinction between these different aspects of behaviour is a difficult one to draw in practice. This is precisely why in badly controlled or poorly conducted experiments it is sometimes possible to produce results which support the 'rules' indicated above. For in these experiments people give the answers they have learnt to regard as correct. An example of this is given by the comment that frequently comes from teachers of design. They say that 'students come into their school unable to deal with colour properly, they use blue to make things seem near or red to relax people, in fact it is two or three years before they can see things as they *really* are!' If things 'really are' any particular way why does it take people (presumably pre-selected for their aesthetic sensibilities) so much training and learning to become aware of them?

QUESTIONS FOR DISCUSSION

(1) If you repeat the rating of photographs experiment described at the beginning of the chapter separately with males and females, do you find any differences from those reported? Why (not)?
(2) What examples can be found in architecture which make use of the following perceptual phenomena? How do these phenomena affect the reactions of people to buildings?
    (a) Contrast
    (b) Constancy

    (c) Figure/ground

    (d) Stevens's Power Law.

(3) How would you carry out an experiment to see if wall colour made rooms look bigger? What is the likely result? Why?

(4) What is the implication of context effects for the organisation of experiments in which a series of judgements are to be made sequentially by each subject?

(5) If the 'golden mean' were to be given experimental support what would this imply for the psychology of perception?

Chapter 4

Learning

4.1. A Relevant Controversy

From the mid-thirties to the mid-forties one of the central battles in psychology was fought in the arena of learning theory. Thousands of publications and experiments were carried out in order to show what the processes were which underlay the ability of man and other animals to learn. Over the years many theories had been developed that attempted to explain and predict learning behaviour and many psychologists devoted their lives to showing that one or other particular theory best fitted the facts. This controversy has died down to a large degree these days partly because of a fading interest amongst psychologists in such polemics and partly because a certain rapprochement has been achieved between the different viewpoints. However, if we take a typical experiment around which these controversies raged it will help us to see the relevance to architecture of the study of learning.

In Figure 4.1 is shown a simple maze of the sort that was designed for use by one of psychology's best friends, the rat. Each of the arms might be six feet long or more. As you can see in the figure, food of some sort is attached to the north end of the maze and so if we were to admit our rat to the east entrance regularly, the chances are he would learn to turn right at the intersection and run north to get the food. In other words, with suitable training the rat will learn the appropriate response that will lead it to its food. Or as psychologists might express it, the correct response is learned because of the reinforcing, rewarding or motivating properties of the food.

Now, having trained our rat, what happens if instead of letting him enter the maze at the east entrance we put him in at the west? What will the animal do at the intersection, assuming that the food is not visible there, will he turn left or right? The answer to this question would help us to understand what sort of processes underlie the learning which has been observed. For instance, if the animal undauntingly turns right at the intersection, thus missing his lunch, then we can say that he has built up a series of stimulus and response connections. He has learnt to carry out a sequence of actions in order to get his food. If on the other hand the animal turns left

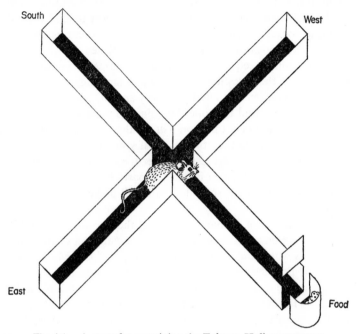

Fig. 4.1. A maze for examining the Tolman–Hull controversy.

we can assume that he has built up some sort of internal representation of the maze (a 'cognitive map') from which he knows that the food is to the north. In other words, the rat's act of turning to the right or to the left when starting from the west entrance helps us to know whether he has learnt a *response* or a *place*. Two of the leading schools of psychology were locked in battle over the behaviour of the rat in this and similar situations. The place learners being led by Tolman[1] and the response learners by Hull.[2]

One of the strengths of this problem lay in the fact that it was open to empirical investigation and (as Mowrer[3] shows) a number of studies were in fact carried out with rather inconclusive findings.

Mowrer goes on to show that these two viewpoints are not necessarily in conflict. Without going in to the complexities of his theorising we can do the same. In our case we need simply to consider an analogous case in the architectural context to that of our hardworking rat. Let us say for instance that you are attending a party in an English semi-detached house and you want to find the toilet but cannot locate the hosts to ask them for instructions. Will you decide in what position the toilet has been placed, or will you go through a familiar sequence of acts in the hope of getting there? Your answer to this question will relate to a large degree on the way in which you have learnt to find your way around houses. If in other houses you have found the toilet by going up the stairs and turning left then it is quite likely that you will try the same series of actions in the present case. On the other hand, if you have worked out that the toilet and bathroom are usually over the kitchen then, provided you know where the kitchen is and the party has not progressed so far that you are totally disoriented, you will make your way to the correct *place*.

Mowrer argues a similar point about the rat in the maze. If the maze is uncovered and hence the rat can get many cues from outside of it (such as where the lights are) then it is possible for him to learn to relate the position of the food to these other cues. In other words if he has been encouraged to learn the general location of the food rather than to learn how to get there, he will behave *as if* he has a 'mental map'. If the rat is however taught that food will always be to the right, say by subsequently admitting him to the maze at the south entrance and placing the food at the east, then it is likely that he will deal with any new entrance position by making the appropriate right-handed response.

Thus one of the crucial points that emerges from these studies is that we learn ways of finding out about our environment. It might even be said that the most important things we learn are how to learn. One consequence of this in buildings is that people may often *not* do what they are expected to because they are being guided by habits or approaches to the building quite different from those the architect had considered.

Let us take another example to illustrate this: a person trying to find the correct platform at a British Railways station. Why, much to the annoyance of the designer who lavished so much money and time on the signposting system, will the traveller so often ask directions of people in uniform? According to our analysis above we can suggest that it is because he has learnt in the past not to trust signs and mechanical indicators, but to deal with the stressful situation by approaching the nearest official.

In some ways then, the study of learning is the analysis of the process by which habits become established. Our central point so far has been that many of the important habits are those which enable us to cope with our environment. But the analysis of learning can also help to explain and predict such behaviour as shopping patterns[4] of immigrants to an area. Typically they will in the first few weeks 'shop around' trying out a variety of places to shop until eventually their behaviour stabilises and they only use two or three shopping areas. They have, in effect, learnt the best place to shop. One implication of this for architecture is that established patterns on the part of building users should only be expected to occur in situations in which previous learning to build up those habits (say of route finding, or equipment use, such as lifts) was possible. In other cases the designer should be able to anticipate a variety of relatively random behaviour in the early use of his building. But this random behaviour will only stabilise if the appropriate *conditions for learning* are present. Thus one of the values of looking at learning theory in the context of buildings is to provide us with a language (or at least a vocabulary) for describing the conditions under which relatively stable patterns of behaviour within buildings will take place. Much of the remainder of this chapter, as a consequence, is devoted to describing aspects of the learning situation. It is not really essential to consider the aspects described as part of fundamental processes within human beings, although many learning theorists would hold this to be the case. Instead we are concerned with developing a precise language which will enable us to describe the conditions under which modification of behaviour takes place.

4.2. Reinforcement

A central concept in understanding the conditions of learning is the concept of reinforcement. Behaviour will only change in relation to any given stimulus if it is reinforced. In other words some increase in satisfaction must result from the behaviour or it will not be learnt. For instance, if you find that a particular library usually has the books you want then you will tend to use that library. The response of going to the library is reinforced by the fact that they have the books. But it must be remembered that the starting point for learning is that you *want* the books. There must be some motivation, some desire to be satisfied, before behaviour leading to a learnt response will take place.

The central role of reward (positive reinforcement), punishment (negative reinforcement) and the eventual disappearance of a response in the absence of continuing reinforcement (response extinction), all fit in to 'common sense' expectations. It is nonetheless the case that a lack of awareness by designers of the importance of reinforcement in behaviour modification often leads them to expect the users of their buildings to learn responses for which the building does not provide reinforcing conditions.

The University of Surrey campus provides a classic example of the absence of awareness of the implications of reinforcement by the provision of tarmac studs placed on the perimeter road as a means of slowing traffic. In learning theory terms the jolts they give to a car are expected to produce negative reinforcement and thus encourage slower driving. However the annoyance also produced is likely to motivate drivers to find ways of coping with these obstacles. Many have thus found that travelling along the road at 35 mph successfully reduces the jolting effect. Now travelling at this speed would only be punished if police checks were possible, which is out of the question on a university perimeter road. As a consequence there is considerable reinforcement for driving quickly along the road especially at night. Casual observations and the number of accidents indicate that of an evening drivers do behave in exactly the opposite way to that which was intended by the designers. Yet the designers have provided conditions for the learning of this unexpected behaviour.

So far we have dealt with reinforcement in only one type of learning, a type these days most closely associated with the name of Skinner.[5] He has called it *operant conditioning* because it is basically the conditioning of an actual operation, or response, through reinforcement. This type of learning is frequently contrasted with *classical* conditioning which is most closely associated with Pavlov[6] and his dogs. In the case of operant conditioning the response which is reinforced is usually produced more or less spontaneously by the organism, but in classical conditioning the response which is eventually conditioned is initially a naturally occurring reflex. For instance if a puff of air is blown on to the eye then the natural reflex is to blink. This blink may be considered in most cases to be an unconditioned response, but if a buzzer were regularly to be sounded shortly before the puff of air was administered then eventually the blink would be produced in response to the buzzer alone. The blink would become a conditioned response. In this case the reinforcement comes from the continued association of the buzzer with the puff of air. The puff of air has reinforcing properties by virtue of its *involuntary* link to the blink.

Consideration of classical conditioning will show why it is sometimes referred to as sign learning. For the process is the association of some response with a signal which 'represents' the initial reinforcing stimulus. The signal thus comes to take on some of the properties of the initial stimulus. It is sometimes possible for these reinforcing properties to be passed on to yet another stimulus, say a tone which precedes the buzzer so that a secondary level of reinforcement may be achieved due to the fact that the buzzer has become capable of 'secondary' reinforcement. An analogous linking procedure frequently occurs with operant conditioning. In this case the previously reinforced response becomes linked to a subsequent stimulus and thus help to produce learning of other responses which follow that stimulus. For instance, if going to the library and finding books is a positively reinforced activity (by books being available) then actually getting the bus to the library may become an activity which is positively reinforced by virtue of the books which are available at the end of the series of acts initiated by getting the bus.

Looking at these two types of linkages helps us to see the similarities between classical and operant conditioning. Indeed the main difference can be summarised by the fact that with classical conditioning stimuli are being learnt and with operant conditioning it is the responses which are learned. Thus it is possible to see why it is that by considering both these aspects of learning, together with the process of secondary reinforcement and stimulus-response chaining, many have suggested that it is possible to explain a great deal of complex human behaviour by reference to learning theory. Language, for instance, is often discussed as a development of the learning of signs through the building up of complex secondary reinforcements. Intricate motor skills such as flying a plane are sometimes described in terms of the building up of associated patterns of learned response.

Of course, there are many arguments against this stand, as can be seen in other chapters. The processes of learning clearly do not explain absolutely all of human behaviour but there are many situations in which they go a long way towards helping us to under-stand why people act as they do.

The general relevance of learning theory to architecture can be best seen if we take our theoretical discussion to a further level of abstraction by considering very briefly the attempt which Mowrer[3] has made to provide a unifying theory for the two types of learning already described. Mowrer suggests that central to all learning processes are emotional reactions. Indeed we may paraphrase him as saying that we learn in essence motivations not responses. Simplifying his ideas a great deal, he sees 'hope' or 'fear' as the actual reinforcing agents in the majority of learning situations. Putting it in lay language we blink in response to the buzzer because we *fear* a puff of air might follow and we go the library because we *hope* we will find there the book which we want.

If we accept this central role for emotional experience in learning then it seems likely that our methods of dealing with buildings, of learning what they are for and what we should do within them, are all likely to have a firm emotional basis. It should not therefore be surprising if people are found to deal most effectively with those buildings or parts of buildings which relate to emotionally potent activities because these activities are most likely to generate strong reinforcements and thus to facilitate learning. For instance we might expect people to learn quickly the best route to a station platform because of the emotional stress of catching a train. On the other hand we might expect people to take considerably longer to find their way around an amusement park.

4.3. Schedules of Reinforcement

An interesting light has been thrown upon the processes of reinforcement by study of the effects of different patterns of reinforcement over time. For instance you may find the book you are looking for every time you go to the library or a book may only be found every third or fourth time, alternatively books may only be found on random occasions or only at the end of each month. If finding the book is considered the primary reinforcement then the question arises if suddenly no more books can be found that you want to read, how long will it be before you stop going to the library altogether (assuming that you don't know definitely that there will be no more suitable books). The answer to this question can be guessed on the basis of studies of much simpler situations, such as animals pressing levers. The more regular the pattern of reinforcement the more quickly will the behaviour cease once the reinforcement is stopped. In other words if reinforcement is intermittent then it is likely that the behaviour will continue long after that reinforcement has stopped altogether. It is this finding which has added great strength to the claims of learning theorists such as Skinner that learning processes underlie the great majority of human activity. For it is apparent that in the world outside of the laboratory, patterns of reinforcement are usually intermittent or irregular and thus behaviour continues for a long time although no apparent reinforcement for it exists.

A pet annoyance of mine may be cited to illustrate this point. In many public buildings the architect has thoughtfully provided double doors; however, for administrative and other unfathomable reasons there is a tendency for one of these doors to be locked. Now if in any building there is a higher likelihood of this being the right-hand one then, although one would develop the habit of opening the left-hand door without thinking, if there were any administrative change such that the left-hand door was now the one which tended to be locked, or if one went to another building which had this alternative policy, then the new habit of opening the right-hand door would be quickly learned. However, what seems to be the case is that an almost, but not quite, random pattern is instituted so that a habit develops of unthinkingly opening, say, the right-hand door. This habit is irregularly reinforced over many months and thus when any change occurs it is extremely difficult to break this habit. One is thus for ever trying to push the right door open when it is locked. The fact that on odd occasions it is indeed unlocked only helps to continue this disturbing response.

4.4. Transfer of Training

A further aspect of learning which relates to our double doors problem is that of the transfer of a learnt response to a given stimulus from one situation to another. The sort of problems associated with this are most apparent in training situations. Let us say for example that a fireman has learnt to leave his bed in the middle of the night and run down the flight of steps to the right of his bedroom in order to reach his fire engine. If he finds himself in a new building where this right turn is no longer appropriate it might be some time before he unlearns the old response and learns the new.

As well as the *negative transfer* which our fireman illustrates it is also possible to have *positive transfer* of training. In this case the new situation in which a person finds himself requires him to respond in a similar way to the stimuli with which he is presented, *i.e.* to the way he responded in an earlier situation. Positive transfer can thus be of considerable value in enabling people to cope adequately with new situations or in enabling people to move quickly between a great variety of them. This is one of the main arguments for standardising the design of many of the aspects of our physical surroundings.

Of importance when examining problems of negative transfer in relation to buildings, is the question of whether it is new (or different) stimuli which require *similar* responses, or similar stimuli which require *different* responses. Quite different strategies will be necessary for coping with these different aspects. Thus in the design of call buttons on lifts having one set of buttons which required you to indicate whether you wished to go up or down, and in the same building call buttons which simply allowed you to indicate that you required a lift, could lead to confusion. In this case the response of pressing the button would be similar but the stimulus presentation (the display panel) would be different. It might be expected in this building that people would either search for the missing button or press either button whether they wished to go up or down. Clearly the strategy most readily available for dealing with this (admittedly minor) conflict would be to change the display conditions to make them similar.

Thus in many cases in which the stimulus conditions are similar but the appropriate responses are different, one modification often available to the designer is to make the stimuli similar. For example at Surrey University, due to the sloping site, the designers have created a system of designating floor levels in relation to sea level or some such. The lowest level is 17 and the highest in the mid 20's. Now this system, needless to say, requires some learning but imagine the confusion when moving to some buildings on the campus and discovering that the conventional system starting at ground floor is used for signposting. The two systems of stimuli (signs) require the same set of responses and thus the fact that they are different leads to considerable negative transfer.

Many other examples, at the building scale as well as that of the urban environment, could be cited. Placing main entrances in the location and configuration which we have learnt to associate with minor entrances; or leading four lane roads into narrow streets, are examples which spring to mind. The reader is encouraged to find others for himself.

The significance of transfer of training helps to highlight the almost involuntary nature (once they have been learned) of many of the responses we have been considering. Although we *know* that a particular response is the most appropriate one in any given situation it is possible that learned reactions may override that knowledge, especially when we are responding quickly ('without thinking'). Consequently, it should be apparent that the processes of learning that we have been considering relate more closely to what is commonly referred to as 'habit' rather than to the understanding of complex concepts which is what is 'learnt' at school. However, it is possible to discuss this latter type of learning from the viewpoint of the principles to which we have referred, as Mowrer[7] for instance shows. Unfortunately such a discussion would take us beyond the level and scope of the present book.

4.5. *Discrimination and Generalisation*

It helps us to understand the nature of learning if we think of two complementary processes underlying it; discrimination and generalisation. On the one hand the person must learn to discriminate between all possible stimuli so that he only responds to those upon which reinforcement is contingent. On the other hand, a learnt response can only play a positive role in adaptation to the environment if the response is generalised to some degree. That is, by occurring in relation to stimuli similar to, but other than, the specific ones which were originally learnt. For example, in a large open office it is not uncommon for people to learn to be undisturbed by a telephone ringing in a different section from their own, although one at the same distance but on a desk within their section will attract attention. In other words they have learnt to discriminate quite accurately between telephone bells on the basis of the position of the telephone. In some respects all learning inevitably involves discrimination because both the stimuli and the responses which are associated through learning were present before learning took place. In order to learn, responses must be associated with *specific* stimuli. These must therefore be discriminated. As a consequence anything which aids discrimination will aid learning and we can see from that the important role in learning which the perceptual processes (discussed in the previous chapter) must play. The ability to distinguish things from their context, for instance, is clearly necessary for learning to take place.

An example of the value of generalisation is provided with reference to the finding of sources of information (such as route finding) in buildings. We certainly do not know innately from where we can get information. We must learn where these people or objects are most likely to be located and how to find them. Now their locations will differ in many ways and so if learning were very specific we would never be able to find our way to the advice bureau in any new building complex; however, by generalisation we can benefit from the others we have experienced.

This example also raises the issue of *gradients of generalisation*. Some universities, say, may have men behind glass screens ready to deal with visitors' queries, others may simply have a proliferation of maps. A hierarchy of similarities could be produced for all these places and we would expect people to find their way most readily around those closest in the hierarchy to their previous experience. Some attempt to clarify the gradients along which generalisations take place in relation to learnt environmental behaviour may well prove invaluable in design.

Finally we may point out that the sort of learnt emotional response most frequently associated with classical conditioning also provides many examples of generalisation. It is possible for instance, that having experienced severe distress in a particular building, say in a church from having attended a funeral service there, that this distress would then generalise to the same building on other occasions, possibly to other similar buildings, perhaps even to all other churches.

4.6. Experience

The essence of this chapter is that we do not approach any new situation in a vacuum but that we bring with us a range of learned responses that enable us to deal with that situation, usually more effectively. Thus any designer of a building or part of a building should not expect that the users of his designs will deal with them as if they were the first designs with which they had had contact. Rather they will respond to them on the basis of the learned patterns they had acquired through contact over the years with similar designs.

This is not as negative a conclusion as it might seem. It does not mean that architects should only produce buildings similar to those which already exist (although it does help to explain why they so often do). What it does mean is that no matter how new the particular form produced the chances are that people will have learned responses that will enable them to deal with the building, or that they will be able to develop them. There is the further possibility that within any particular building the architect can, through the intelligent use of the ideas discussed in this chapter, quickly enable the building users to learn the appropriate responses. For instance, the repetition of specific relationships, such as between a particular activity and the location of the room which houses that activity, may 'teach' people how the building is used and thus enable them to use it more effectively.

An interesting light is thrown on the implications of learning if we think of it as the inculcation of a state of readiness in the person who has learned. In other words, past experience gives rise to a reduction in the range of likely reactions to future ones. Thus if a particular stimulus commonly occurs in relation to a given response then we 'expect' the response to follow the stimulus. Such expectations may well be the basis of formal developments within architecture and provide the groundwork for many 'styles' ancient and modern.

The learning theories which we have been discussing help to reveal some of the patterns of previous experience which are crucial for producing a learnt response. For instance, it should now be apparent that emotional reinforcements can play a critical part in determining our responses to buildings. At a more rational level the relationships which we expect between actions and displays, such as in learning to operate machinery, can be seen to relate directly to learning experiments like those conducted with animals. Indeed an important area of ergonomics which deals with display and control systems draws heavily upon learning theory (see Figure 4.2 for some examples).

Within all this, such matters as the schedules of reinforcement, and discrimination learning are relevant because they provide the designer with guidelines which would enable the users of his buildings to learn how to behave within them more effectively. Suddenly changing critical relationships could have a far larger effect than would be expected if one did not consider the learnt responses, which had been associated with those relationships.

More detailed consideration of theoretical issues may also prove fruitful in the design of buildings. If, for instance, we were to examine the place/response controversy with which we started this chapter, it is possible that quite different designs would be produced by people taking different sides of the controversy. A response learner could follow a simple sequence of left–right–left turns more readily than a complex sequence whereas a place learner would deal with a simple structured map (e.g. a circle), no matter how complex the route.

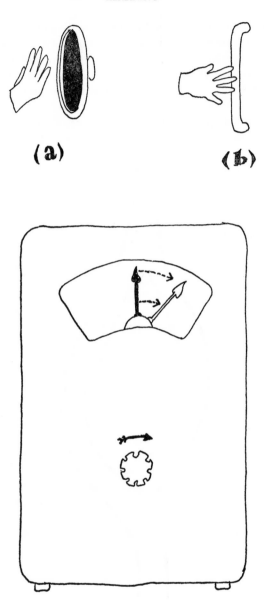

Fig. 4.2. Expected display and control relationships.

The further possibility we raised that the building or set of buildings experienced can give rise to a particular mode of learning might go a long way to explain why Americans brought up in cities with grid iron plans get so easily lost in European cities and *vice versa*. Both groups have learnt a different way of learning or finding their way around a city.

A final question we must raise is the one of reinforcement. We have really not said much about its intrinsic nature. A common

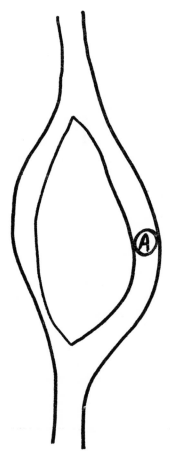

Figure 4.3.

assumption is that all primary reinforcers satisfy fundamental physiological needs and thus secondary reinforcers are really based on these. Such notions as altruism can only find an uncomfortable place in this system. However, an intriguing definition of art is to define it as something which has reinforcing properties (in other words we will learn to repeat the experience of it) but for which no specific function can be found. This of course raises many problems but one interesting possibility is that a building, or part of a building, may be rewarding in its own right (*i.e.* without reference to 'more primary' reinforcers). If these reinforcing aspects of buildings could be isolated then the possibility of using buildings as an integral part of the learning process would be very great indeed.

QUESTIONS FOR DISCUSSION

(1) Examine those instances in which you use some route or aspect of the environment habitually, although it is not necessarily the best route or way of using the environment. What were the conditions for learning these habits?

(2) Taking a pair of paths similar to those illustrated in Figure 4.3, what would you need to introduce at A in order to modify the patterns of movement along those paths. Why?

(3) In what situations would you consider it valuable to encourage negative transfer of training in buildings? Why? How would you do it?

(4) Select a particular stimulus-response link expected in buildings (either small scale, such as opening doors, or large scale such as place selection) and identify the hierarchy of similarities for these links. How could you make use of these in considering designs?

(5) How would you carry out an experiment to find out if New Yorkers use different processes to find their way around unfamiliar places than Londoners? What results would you expect and why?

Chapter 5

Development

5.1. The Study of Development

An important proportion of the resources of any society is devoted to turning children into civilised, contributing members of that society. Many more groups and institutions have as their main reason for existence the need to help, protect, encourage or heal children so that they will become healthy adults. Thus we have families, educational institutions, youth organisations, medical services and a great variety of manufacturing and service industries geared to children. This has two important implications for us.

The first is the assumption underlying all these activities that children are different from adults. The second is the need to produce a great variety of buildings to house these institutions. The combination of these two is the pressing need by architects to understand the ways in which children differ from adults. That all the above is obvious, raises the question of why in the training of architects little, if any, consideration is given to these matters.

A brief comparison of two recently built children's hospitals may help to illustrate the implications of examining these issues. The new children's hospital in Glasgow[1] was designed in close collaboration with the senior medical and nursing staff. As a consequence each ward has a similar plan and the hospital appears to be conceived and organised according to medical specialities, children being assigned to wards on the basis of their illness. By contrast, for the new children's hospital in Palo Alto[2] the design team determined to draw as fully as they could upon prevailing information in developmental psychology. The building they produced is organised upon the basis of the differences between children of different ages. Children are, in the main, placed in a particular part of the hospital in relation to their age rather than their illness.

Whether or not the psychological research literature is best interpreted in the way the Stanford designers did is open to considerable discussion but the comparison does emphasise one of the basic findings which the psychological study of children has helped to clarify, a finding which most parents or teachers heartily endorse, namely that children of different ages are very different. In fact, if you wanted to find one measurement which would enable you to account most readily for differences between people, chronological age would be your best bet. Almost all aspects of behaviour can be shown to relate to age (Bromley[3]). This is not surprising, because age relates closely to many other important determinants of behaviour such as physical development and role in society. It is therefore only to be expected that psychologists should have paid considerable attention to this aspect of differences between people. What is possibly more surprising is that attention in the main has been directed to the way in which people develop in the early years of life, rather than to the way in which people mature over the later years (although this is changing, *e.g.* Eisdorfer and Lawton[4]).

Furthermore, possibly because the variations are there for all to see and because the problems are so central to the scientific study of people, by far the biggest impact on the scientific study of behaviour has come from the understanding of child development. Most well known psychologists have made contributions which are most directly pertinent to understanding how a child becomes an adult. Pavlov, Freud and Skinner all have specified, as a central part of their theories, mechanisms which help to explain the processes, either within the child or his environment, which shape his behaviour. However, the central role of developmental psychology in psychology in general can best be illustrated with reference to the work of Piaget. Although for most of this century he has been concerned directly with the study of children of all ages, and from actual empirical observations he has developed a theory of development of great power and breadth, his contribution to psychology has been much wider and it seems likely that his work will come to be accepted as the most significant psychological research this century.

5.2. Nature versus Nurture

Besides providing an understanding of how children develop and change, developmental psychology can also provide us with insights as to the causes and origins of those changes. It is clear, for example, that some human characteristics are innate, that is, they are determined to a large degree by inheritance. Many physical, racial characteristics, for instance, or hair and eye colour are inherited. On the other hand, it is clear that some aspects of behaviour are learned and that they develop through an interaction with the environment (the language a person speaks relates to the language with which he had most contact). Thus because there are these two types of major determinants of behaviour, it is important to discover for any specific aspect of behaviour the degree to which it is environmentally or genetically determined. As we shall see, by examining human development, we may be able to clarify some of these determinants of behaviour. This is of theoretical importance because it has far reaching implications for our understanding of the underlying mechanisms which control behaviour. If an aspect of behaviour, say intelligence, is found to be largely determined by heredity, then it is likely that it has some specific biochemical or physiological basis which is passed genetically from one generation to the next. From a practical viewpoint this means that modification is limited to the range that the genetic structure allows.

Establishing the main determinants of behaviour has most relevance in architecture in relation to responses to specific environmental stimuli. If, for instance, there were innate tendencies to move towards the brighter part of any space then architects could use this tendency in a very specific way to manipulate behaviour. Many of the ideas which together are described under the heading of 'architectural determinism' (Lee[5]) can be shown to have their origins in the belief that many aspects of human response to the environment are innate. Similarly if an architect believed that people had few innate propensities but that all behaviour is moulded by the environment, with little possibility of people reacting independently of their surroundings, then once again he would hold an extreme determinist view. The architect would doubtless believe that he had only to discover the secrets of these processes of control in order to produce the type of responses, or indeed people that he wanted, and that he would manipulate people through the buildings he produced.

Assumptions about the underlying determinants of behaviour

thus have a crucial influence over a wide range of human activities. There are two basic ways in which these assumptions can be tested. Either people who are genetically similar but who have experienced different environments are studied. Or the process of development over time is observed. The former usually consists of the study of twins comparing those which have been brought up together, with those which have been brought up apart or monozygotic with dyzygotic twins (Claridge et al.[6]). The latter forms a major part of child psychology.

The picture which is beginning to emerge from developmental studies is that there is an intricate interaction between innate tendencies and environmental possibilities so that extreme points of view in the nature/nurture controversy are rarely found amongst psychologists today. The person who has done most to emphasise and elucidate this interaction is Piaget.

5.3. Piaget's Theories

Jean Piaget first started publishing shortly before World War I and he has published continually since. Over these years his ideas have developed and expanded and so it is possible to give only an indication of the scope of his work in a few pages. It is worth while presenting a few of his basic theoretical concepts and indicating their possible relevance to architecture in the hope that the reader will be encouraged to spend the time reading more detailed accounts (such as those listed at the end of this book).

But first we should look at a typical Piaget experiment. The aim of the experiment is to see how the child handles concepts of the world about him so that his responses can be compared with children of different ages. For instance, a seven-year-old child may be given a ball of clay and asked to make another of the same size and shape. When the child is satisfied that the two balls are the same size the experimenter changes the shape of one of them, say by chopping it up into smaller pieces, or by rolling it out in a sausage shape. The child is then questioned to see if he still thinks the modified clay has the same weight, volume or mass as the other piece. By further questioning and manipulation of the clay, the investigator establishes the limits of the child's understanding of the relationship between weight, volume, mass and shape. The general finding in this type of study is that in the early years there is no *conservation*. That is, change of shape induces the child to think that a change of weight has been produced. However there comes a time when the child accepts the invariance of weight across shapes and thus can be said to have established some form of cognitive constancy in relating these properties.

Another experiment indicates a similar point. A 5 or 6 year old is shown two rows of six counters laid out in a line with equal spaces between them so that the two rows can be related one to one. He is asked to count them and make sure he agrees that there are the same number in each row. When he agrees, one of the rows is extended so the number of counters is the same but the length of each row is different. On questioning it is found that the child does not think that there are the same number of counters because the lines are of unequal length.

It is important to realise that these studies and the thousands of others carried out with children of all ages, are thought of as examinations of the child's cognitive structure not tests of the efficiency of his perceptual processes. The aim of the investigations is first to isolate those aspects of cognitive functioning which are invariant across ages and, secondly, to describe the common developmental stages.

One problem is whether stages in development really can be discerned, with distinct changes from one to the next, or whether a smooth progression takes place. The answer which seems to be emerging is that for certain aspects of behaviour, such as cognitive processes, there are radically different changes in rate of development which indicate the presence of distinct stages. For other aspects, such as response to visual illusions, a much more gradual series of changes can be observed. The detailed answers to these questions could have far reaching architectural implications, particularly for the design of accommodation for children. It would help architects to decide if they should provide different types of accommodation for children of different ages, at what age (or stage) something different should be provided, and where the important differences might lie.

5.4. Adaptation

A concept central to Piaget's understanding of development is that of adaptation. He sees an intricate series of adaptations taking place which each in turn lead to a stable level of equilibrium. The form which this equilibrium takes differs from age to age and really is defined in terms of the stage of development at which the child is.

This process of adaptation is made up of two complementary components. The person either *assimilates* aspects of the environment into the set of cognitive structures he already has, or he *accommodates* those structures in order to incorporate some novel aspect of his surroundings. The type and balance of these two aspects of adaptation give rise to the distinctive features of any particular stage of development. The imbalance between the processes leads to subsequent levels of integration and the appropriate equilibrium.

A simple example of these two processes in action may help to clarify them. Say, for instance, an infant is shown for the first time a ring hanging on a string. The chances are he will look at it, try and grasp it or possibly even make it swing. These actions are primitive forms of accommodation in that the child is modifying its behaviour in order to make the ring relate to the actions of which it is capable. As a consequence of previous experience, he already has some sort of cognitive structure to which he must assimilate his present actions. In doing this he must modify those structures to some degree. As Flavell[7] puts it 'the child's actions with respect to the ring are at once accommodation of these concepts or structures to the reality contours of the ring and assimilations of this new object to these concepts'.

A more clear-cut example of assimilation is fantasy play (say, making a playmate out of a cardboard box). In this case, the real world properties of the object are distorted (perhaps momentarily) to fit in with the child's cognitions. By contrast the nearest one can get to a pure example of accommodation is mimicking. In this case the child is, say, producing noises which, whilst having little meaning in his own cognitive structure relate closely to things happening externally to him.

In the first two years or so of life it is difficult to differentiate clearly between assimilation and accommodation. The child's reactions show little distinction between *the child's* own actions and those of others. By the end of this stage, referred to as the period of 'sensori-motor intelligence', the child has developed the cognitive structures that enable him to deal with objects (or the actions of others) as distinct from himself. He acts as if he and the people with whom he interacts each have an independent existence. He can also deal with physical objects in the same way. Whereas at birth the infant and his world are so inextricably mixed that he can only react to the existence of something if he is directly experiencing it, by the end of this stage he has moved to an equilibrium level that gives his world the permanence and stability in which language develops. This is still only a stability in terms of sensations and motor actions. It will be some years before the child is able to deal with concepts in the same way.

An interesting aspect of this development, which recurs at different levels of sophistication throughout child development, is that it is through the differentiation of self and others, or self and objects, that the child becomes less egocentric. It is, for instance, through the development of a stable physical world that the child is able to respond to a world that is independent of himself.

The second major period may be thought of as encompassing the years from two to about eleven. As in the first two years a tremendous variety of developments take place but very briefly these may be thought of as the organisation of 'concrete operations'. To quote Flavell[7] again: 'The invariance which the sensori-motor period won for the whole object the concrete-operational period wins for its attributes'. The representations which the child has of the world about him, whether they be verbal or non verbal, take on a stability and coherence which was almost totally absent at the beginning of this period.

This major period is usually dealt with as containing two clearly distinct sub-periods, the pre-operational period up to the seventh or eighth year and the period of concrete operations proper after that. In the former stage the child's conceptions relate to acts performed on the object; it is only after the pre-operational stage that the child can deal with the object independently of what has been done to it. To illustrate this distinction with another conservation example. In the pre-operational stage children will think the quantity of water has changed when it is poured from a long thin jar to a small fat one. In the stage of concrete operations this is no longer the case.

The final period with which Piaget deals is usually thought of as leading to a higher order equilibrium in late adolescence. It is called the period of 'formal operations'. During this period the child stabilises the operations he can perform upon the representations that were stabilised by the end of the second period. This ability to perform formal operations consistently is the basis of the kind of mature adult thought which is essential for scientific activity. The child can now perform the various transformations of the attributes clarified in the period of concrete operations in a consistent and reversible manner. In order to explain this development in detail Piaget finds he has to use mathematical procedures taken from symbolic logic and group theory.

For our purposes we can perhaps clarify the achievements of this later stage by the following example. At the beginning of this stage a child presented with a picture of a blackbird and told that all crows are black birds will insist that this black bird must be a crow. At the end of the stage the child can deal with the argument in the abstract, he can deal with the possible as well as the actual. As a consequence he can consider the form of the argument as well as its content, and thus indicate that perhaps the photograph is not a crow after all.

Hopefully a glimmering of the implications for the psychological study of buildings should now be apparent. In the first place Piaget shows that there are basic mechanisms that are inherent to the human organism but that these mechanisms evolve and develop through the interaction of the organism with its environment. Heredity places people in a positive interactive role *vis à vis* their surroundings but these surroundings also help to modify the way in which that role develops. Architects, therefore, cannot assume that people will enter their buildings with certain inherent propensities to react in certain ways, nor can they assume that they may be moulded willy nilly. Rather the architect must realise the buildings will to some degree determine the way people will interact with those buildings but whether the architect wishes it or not it will always be an *interaction* never simply a reaction.

From the point of view of buildings for children there seem to be at least two specific implications. Firstly that at quite an early age children can make 'sense' (at a sensori-motor level) of their physical surroundings. They can probably, therefore, find their way around complex configurations of space and deal with changes which many adults possibly think of as too complex for such a young mind. The second implication is with regard to the study of children's response to their environments. We must wait until the end of the stage of concrete operations before we can really expect to gain anything like a valid account of their experience of a building; before that time we can only examine the distortions of the child's view of things in relation to the developmental stages through which he is progressing.

There thus seems to be evidence for the surmise that early activities within particular buildings give rise to a range of mechanisms for dealing with those buildings. It is probable that even at the early sensori-motor level we develop habits for dealing with the physical spaces we encounter. These habits possibly provide the basis for many later concepts and attitudes towards buildings. As a consequence a detailed examination of child development through the eyes of Piaget and his collaborators could have far reaching implications for our understanding of the fundamental processes behind adult interaction with the built environment.

5.5. Perceptual Development

With Piaget we have concentrated on the general principles of *cognitive* development but there have been over the past few years a growing number of studies of the way in which very young children *perceive* the world. These studies have lead to changes in our view of the infant's perceptual experiences with a consequent broadening of our understanding of adult perception.

5.5.1. THE VISUAL CLIFF.—Probably the most important of these studies have been those by Walk and Gibson.[8] They developed the situation illustrated in Figure 5.1. Two sheets of plate glass are placed over two different textured surfaces with a slightly raised centreboard

Fig. 5.1. The visual cliff.

between them. One of the surfaces is placed directly under the glass and the other at some distance below it. An infant, usually at the stage of crawling, is placed on the centreboard so that it is possible for him to crawl on to either of the glass surfaces. Walk[9] found that more than 90 % of infants from the ages of $6\frac{1}{2}$ to 15 months avoided the deep side of this visual cliff. However, younger children can be coaxed across the deep side especially if the texture does not enhance the distance illusion, for instance by being diffuse. From these studies it is clear that this important perceptual ability has developed by a very early age, although it is not clear whether this is an innate ability or one which develops through learning in the first six months of life. Various studies with animals have indicated that it is an ability which is present very early in life and which requires very little training to demonstrate.

Recently, a number of investigators have also examined what elicits the attention of newborn babies. Fantz[10] for instance, has carried out a series of studies in which he presents pairs of stimuli to infants and measures the amount of time they look at (or 'visually fixate') each of the stimuli. If one stimulus is looked at more than another then this indicates that the child can discriminate between the stimuli and that in some sense it 'prefers' one to the other. Fantz has thus been able to show that there are specific properties of stimuli which encourage infants to attend to them even in the first weeks of life. Other investigators such as Haith,[11] Spears[12] and Hershenson[13] together with further studies by Fantz himself[14] have made it possible to list those properties which are important for capturing the infant's attention. One of the most central is the complexity of the stimulus. Although complexity has not yet been satisfactorily specified such things as the number of internal contours and the variety of shapes within the stimulus seem to be important aspects of it. Interestingly enough in some cases there appears to be a peak for complexity above or below which attention is not so sustained (Karmel[15]). Other stimulus properties that have been isolated as of importance in fostering attention have been movement, brightness and solidity. Whether these are more validly thought of as all just aspects of complexity remains to be determined by further study. It is also interesting that the human face is one object frequently in the child's field of view which best combines all these properties and, as Fantz[16] has argued very cogently, the early emergence of the infant's preference for attending to certain sorts of stimuli probably contributes to the development of sociability.

The evidence is thus mounting to indicate that we are born into the world with quite a sophisticated set of potential reactions. Provided we have the right sort of environment these potentialities can develop into a complex repertoire of responses at a very early age. The full implication of this for the design of buildings will only be established after many years of research, but it already seems likely that a specific set of reactions to the physical world develops early on and that later developments can only be understood as elaborations of these early responses.

I am not suggesting however that the elaboration of these processes will be straightforward. There is already evidence that some quite major changes in perception occur during the course of development. For instance, Brian and Goodenough in 1929[17] and more recently Corah[18] have shown that when children of four or five years old are asked to indicate which of two stimuli are similar to a third they tend to select the stimulus which is the same colour. When the same task is given to seven or eight year olds they tend to choose the one which is the same form even if it has a different colour. Klein[19] also showed that given the task of matching objects by touch, younger children matched on texture whereas older children matched on shape. Indeed the optical illusions, with which psychologists are so fond of playing, can be divided into those which have an increasing effect with age and those which have a decreasing effect (*see* Pick and Pick[20]).

5.6. Environmental Deprivation

One of the recurrent themes in the studies we have discussed so far has been the effects of early interactions with the environment on later ones. A corollary of this theme is that various forms of deprivation in the environment during the early stages of development can lead to instability and abnormality in later life. The studies relevant to this topic have been discussed most lucidly by Bowlby[21] and Schaffer[22] but they received a notable impetus from the work of Harlow.[23]

Harlow carried out a number of studies in which he compared monkeys reared separately from their own mothers with those reared normally with them. In many experiments he provided surrogate mothers made out of wire. Some of these wire mothers were covered in cloth and it was found that the infant monkey spent more time with the cloth mothers than with the wire ones. Whilst this is of interest in indicating the possibility of early textural preferences in primates, a more important finding from the studies was that the social behaviour of the animals when they became adults was much poorer than that of the animals reared normally. Furthermore, when these animals eventually had children of their own they were very poor mothers indeed.

Harlow also found that ability to deal with the environment even when young related to the presence or absence of a 'mother', even though it was a surrogate mother. The possible relevance of this latter finding to humans has been indicated by the study of

Ainsworth *et al.*[24] who showed that the exploratory behaviour of one year olds was much greater in the presence of the mother than in her absence. The actual role of maternal deprivation in influencing later behaviour has still to be clarified but one interesting point to which Schaffer draws attention is the way in which the mother can provide the infant with a level of stimulation particularly suited to that infant. Whether or not the physical environment similarly needs to provide various forms of stimulation at an optimum level for different individuals has not yet been established but the possibility is certainly worth considering.

5.7. Conclusion

In this chapter we have dealt with one of the most exciting and richest areas not only of scientific psychology but also of common experience. However, many readers may feel that the real excitements of watching a child grow up have been lost in this rather abstract discussion of cognition and perception. Such a feeling is partly due to the fact that we have left the area of social and emotional development unexplored. Besides the fact that anyone interested in these topics can get an excellent account of them from books such as those listed for further reading at the end of the book, it is also my belief that architects usually do not appreciate the relevance of developmental psychology because they get too close to it; too involved, if you will, in the poetry of childhood rather than its practice. It is therefore necessary to take a broader, more abstract view as a starting point.

This chapter has shown that design could only influence behaviour in so far as early experience or innate potentialities allowed. Furthermore, it has indicated that children interact with the environment in different ways at different stages of their development and are therefore likely to demand different things of it at those stages. However, it is likely that at all stages some sort of balance, whether it be Piaget's balance of assimilation and accommodation or an optimum level of stimulation, is one of the central requirements.

QUESTIONS FOR DISCUSSION

(1) Do children of different ages require different amounts of space in which to play? Why?

(2) What differences between people who had grown up in the city or the country might be expected in their reactions to multi-storey dwellings? Why?

(3) What aspects of response to the built environment are innate? How do you know?

(4) In a public building, in what would you expect children to take most interest?

(5) Under what conditions do you think toddlers would feel lost in a large room full of toys?

(6) Do you think a children's hospital should be organised according to the age of the children? What about a youth club? How about a sports club or an educational institute for adults?

(7) Look at the architect's view of a children's hospital described in Reference 1. How would an understanding of developmental psychology have influenced it? How would it have influenced the building produced?

Chapter 6

Underlying Dimensions

6.1. An Interesting Discovery

If you take a number of objects, photographs of buildings, people, or they could be just descriptions of objects, people or buildings, and you have these rated using a large number of adjectives, an interesting pattern emerges. No matter what the instructions to the raters the adjectives will not be used independently of one another. In other words, if you sort out the adjectives according to the way in which they are used (for instance if you put together all those adjectives which people use to describe both object A and object B) you will find that many are used in a similar way. If you think of these relationships simply as putting all the adjectives which are used in the same way into one group and all the adjectives which are used in different ways into other groups, you will find, depending on your criteria for forming groups, that there are far fewer groups than you might expect and that quite a large proportion of the adjectives form two or three main groups. This categorisation of adjectives seems to work whether you do it separately for each individual who carries out the original rating or whether you do it with averages for a whole group of people.

The interesting discovery that you could organise descriptions into fairly simple groupings was first shown consistently by Osgood et al.[1] Osgood himself did not really think of his categorisation as groupings but rather as arranging the descriptions according to underlying dimensions. The easiest way of coming to understand what is meant by 'underlying dimensions' is by considering Osgood's early ideas about the meaning of words. He says that when he was still quite young he thought of Roget's *Thesaurus* as 'a vivid and colourful image of words as clusters of starlike points in an immense space'. This idea seems to have re-emerged in a more scientific form following his study of synesthesia. This is the technical name for a frequently occurring aspect of language; the use of descriptions from one sense modality for sensations from a different one. For instance, we talk of a very soft light or of a grating noise, some music is regarded as very colourful, other music is accepted as being cool. The list of examples could go on for ever because it appears that this semantic transfer is the essence of much that we refer to as metaphor. It is not a great leap to assume that these different descriptions although drawn from different areas of sensation all refer to experiences, or concepts, which are common to the different modalities. These common concepts may be thought of as underlying dimensions. That is, theoretical lines drawn through 'clusters of starlike points in an immense space' that help to give that space a structure and to provide us with lines for plotting locations within it.

Of course these guidelines are only of value if they really do organise reasonably large proportions of the space in which we are interested, and it is an empirical problem to find a reasonably small number of lines that will give us maximum guidance. It was the developments in advanced statistics that gave Osgood and others the possibility of actually searching for these underlying dimensions in real data. The aspect of statistics of relevance here is often referred to as multi-variate statistics because it enables us to examine the inter-relationships of a large number of variables at the same time. The earliest procedures to be widely used to search for underlying dimensions usually went under the general heading of factor analysis. I shall concentrate on this procedure here although there are now many others available. The full mathematical details of these procedures (*see*, for instance, Harman[2]) are beyond the scope of this book but it is worth while giving some outline of the processes involved.

Factor analysis starts with a matrix of associations, or relationships. This matrix can be produced in a number of different ways but by far the most common is to inter-correlate all the different words being used and to take these correlations as the initial matrix.

The process of inter-correlation is based upon the way in which people use the words in question when describing various objects or concepts. In order to formalise this process of description so that numbers may be put on it from which correlations may be drawn, people are usually required either to rank the concepts on each of the words being studied (usually adjectives) or they are asked to assign a number to each concept as an indication of the degree to which it possesses the quality expressed by the adjective. Over the years it has been found that this latter process of rating works most effectively if two ends of the adjectival description are specified, *e.g.* good–bad, happy–sad. The reasons why we might expect that presenting the adjectives in this bipolar form would be more valid relate both to the fact that if a person knows what both ends of the scale he is using are, then he is more likely to use that scale in an intelligent and consistent fashion, and to the fact that dealing with things in an *either/or* way (*e.g.* dealing with them as either good or bad) is quite common.

If the division between the two ends of the scale is divided into distinct sections then a degree of precision in the numerical processes involved can be achieved when each of these divisions is assigned a separate value. The actual number of categories is usually determined on quite pragmatic grounds. It depends on how many categories people seem to be able to use and on the size of the computer which is analysing the data. Warr[3] has shown that the number of categories does not really affect the results when typical descriptions and concepts are employed. Generally speaking, however, it has been found that a seven point scale is the most useful.

If then, we take a series of bipolar adjectival scales which have seven point divisions and ask people to use them to rate a series of concepts or objects then we have what is sometimes referred to as a *semantic differential*. Technically, however, it is only really appropriate to refer to sets of scales derived or descended directly from Osgood's work by this term. Such an instrument, as developed particularly for use in the architectural context, is shown in Table 6.1. If properly presented then it is usually found to be quite an interesting exercise and a large number of ratings can be collected. All the ratings on any one scale for all the concepts are then correlated with each of the sets of ratings for every other scale. This provides the correlations of every scale with every other scale which are used as the basic matrix for the factor analysis.

There are many different mathematical procedures for carrying out factor analysis (one of the most commonly used distinct forms being called principal component analysis) but they all have in common an attempt to represent the relationships in the correlation matrix in a limited number of dimensions. The easiest way to think of this process is geometrically. If the relationship between two variables A and B is thought of as a distance such that the more closely related they are the nearer they are in space, then it can be seen that a particular relationship between these two can be expressed as points along a line. If we accept that this line is an underlying

Table 6.1

An example of a 'semantic-differential' type scale as developed for use with buildings [4]

Instructions: This questionnaire has been developed to measure your reactions *in general* to slides. Please indicate where these come on *each* of the scales below by circling the appropriate number (1 to 7). Do not ponder too long over any one question. Please treat each response separately, any apparent repetition of questions is for statistical control. Please ensure you have completed *every* item.

Adequate	1	2	3	4	5	6	7	Inadequate
Suitable	1	2	3	4	5	6	7	Unsuitable
Acceptable	1	2	3	4	5	6	7	Unacceptable
Pleasant	1	2	3	4	5	6	7	Unpleasant
Comfortable	1	2	3	4	5	6	7	Uncomfortable
Good	1	2	3	4	5	6	7	Bad
Interesting	1	2	3	4	5	6	7	Uninteresting
Stimulating	1	2	3	4	5	6	7	Depressing
Best possible	1	2	3	4	5	6	7	Worst possible
Above average	1	2	3	4	5	6	7	Below average

dimension then we can see that the relationships between two points can be expressed in one dimension. If we now take the relationships between three points, A, B and C, then it is clear that mathematically two dimensions are necessary in order to represent completely all three relationships between the variables. Generally speaking if we have *n* variables then we need $n - 1$ dimensions in order to express all the relationships between those variables mathematically.

If we now think back to the correlation matrix produced from the semantic differential, we will realise that although mathematically we might need $n - 1$ dimensions (*n* being the number of adjectives) to account for all the relationships, psychologically it is possible to represent the associations drawn from the way people use the words in far fewer dimensions. This is what the process of factor analysis enables us to do. It enables us to find a small number of dimensions that will reasonably account for the relationships being studied.

In order to find out what these underlying dimensions are, and to put labels on to them for ease of use, it is necessary to decide what all the variables which are highly related to any particular dimension have in common. It may now be realised that this is not so very different from deciding what a cluster of related descriptions have in common, which was one of the original problems at which we looked. There is in fact a great deal of difference statistically between cluster analysis and factor analysis; in the former each variable is placed in only one cluster whereas in the latter all variables have loadings on all dimensions. However, at a simple level, the interesting discovery we discussed at the beginning of this chapter can be rephrased as the finding that only three or four underlying dimensions are usually necessary to explain the relationships between a large number of descriptions.

6.2. The Nature of Underlying Dimensions

The dimensions which are produced by the processes described above are, of course, entirely dependent on the scales which are used by the subjects in the first instance. You only get out what you put in. If there are no words dealing with happiness, joy or merriment, then it is not possible for a dimension of 'jollity' to be produced. Considerable trouble, therefore, goes into the consideration of the words to be used in any study in order to ensure that they are representative of the population being considered.

As we have already seen, Osgood was very interested in language. He was trying to find those dimensions which underlie many of the descriptions we use. His main concern was with the emotional or connotative descriptions. He felt that denotative descriptions, such as red and black, were likely to have quite specific dimensions relating to the properties they describe. In other words, they were nearer to being concepts to be described than descriptions. Osgood therefore selected a representative sample of connotative descriptions from a thesaurus.

His analysis of these words showed three distinct dimensions. The first was one of evaluation, which relates to words like good–bad, pleasant–unpleasant and valuable–worthless; the second was potency: strong–weak, large–small, and heavy–light; the third was activity: active–passive, fast–slow, hot–cold. The analysis he used produces dimensions at right angles to one another. This means that the dimensions are taken as unrelated to one another. It is possible and increasingly more fashionable to produce oblique dimensions but these are more difficult to interpret because it is necessary to take into account relationships between dimensions. With evaluation, potency and activity then we have three general independent dimensions underlying connotative descriptions. It is also possible to say that generally speaking the evaluative dimension is much larger than the other two. In terms of factor analysis this means that it helps to explain a larger proportion of the relationships between the different variables than the other two dimensions. At a more general level we might say that it is more important, central or frequently used when describing things. Although this finding comes out of a series of complex statistical processes it can still be loosely validated against everyday experience. If you listen to any descriptions, other than simple physical accounts, which are made around you during the day, you will notice that a very large proportion of them relate to whether the thing being described is good or bad.

Following from the original semantic differential studies a great number of research workers in many parts of the world, in many different languages, have repeated Osgood's results.[5] This gives strong support to the idea that these three dimensions really do represent three important and commonly occurring aspects of the meaning of words. Besides its theoretical interest and the light it throws upon semantics, this finding has great practical value. It means that if we want to examine a person's feelings about a series of things, instead of getting him to rate them on all the adjectival scales we can think of, we only need to select a few scales highly loaded on each dimension and use them as representatives of the universe of adjectives. The nine pairs of adjectives in the paragraph above are frequently used to form such a scale. It is these nine pairs of adjectives, or a set of adjectives selected in a similar way, which is most accurately described as a 'semantic differential'.

6.3. Dimensions for Architecture

The process described above for producing a semantic differential is commonly used in psychology for selecting a variety of items to use as measures of key dimensions. For instance, most intelligence tests are produced in a similar way. Instead of selecting words from a thesaurus, a large number of test items which are assumed to measure important aspects of intelligence are collected together and given to a large number of children. On the basis of the dimensional analysis of their answers, items which represent the main dimensions are selected.

In the case both of the semantic differential and of intelligence tests there is a distinct universe of items within which it is wished to discover dimensions. What might such a universe consist of in architecture? It might be simply the physical descriptions of buildings. If, for instance, a number of buildings, perhaps selected at random from a population of buildings, were measured on a large number of physical variables (height, materials, deterioration, etc.), then the analysis of these measurements might well give us a new way of categorising buildings. Unfortunately nobody has yet attempted this intriguing exercise, but a study concentrating on the location of classrooms[6] has shown that it is likely to be fruitful. The exercise which has been attempted by a number of people has been to find the dimensions underlying the attitudes people have towards buildings. This type of study is directly analogous to the semantic differential studies. The critical differences are that on the one hand the descriptions are selected from the words which people use to describe or comment on buildings, either in day to day conversation or in published accounts and, on the other hand, instead of using a great range of concepts like 'war' and 'snow' as Osgood did, actual buildings or some representation of them are used.

As might be expected when using so much more limited material the dimensions which are found are not the same as Osgood's. In fact some critics might suggest that precisely because Osgood's dimensions are found so generally they can have little value in any specific situation. They can only be used for studying language in a broad way. However, the architectural dimensions produced do bear some relationship to Osgood's. They all seem to be sub-divisions of his evaluative dimension, activity sometimes being found and potency infrequently occurring as a status dimension. By far the largest and most frequently found dimension is, not surprisingly, one of 'pleasantness' (Canter,[7] Vielhauer,[8] Herschberger[9]). This contains such adjectives as pleasant–unpleasant, beautiful–ugly, interesting–uninteresting, impressive–unimpressive, and characterful–characterless. The other dimensions that commonly occur are those of tidiness (tidy–untidy, harmonious–discordant, coherent–incoherent), of friendliness (friendly–unfriendly, welcoming–unwelcoming, soft–hard) and of comfort (comfortable–uncomfortable, tense–relaxed, cramped–spacious). Items from these dimensions have been selected and related to other variables. A considerable amount of work has been carried out with the friendliness dimension and it has been shown to relate to such things as roof angle, window and furniture arrangement (Canter and Wools[10]).

The pleasantness dimension has been developed into a standard ten item questionnaire which has been used recently in a number of studies (Building Performance Research Unit,[11] Canter and Thorne[12]). It has been found, for instance, to relate closely to the age of a school building[11] and is the questionnaire illustrated in Table 6.1. The value of this type of questionnaire in architecture can only grow with time. For as data are accumulated from these standard questionnaires so more and more comparable information can be gathered. Cross cultural comparisons can be made[13] as there seems to be some generality to the pleasantness dimension like that which Osgood found for his evaluation, potency and activity. Such comparisons would tell us the advantages and disadvantages of producing the same sort of buildings all over the world as we are at the present time. Different investigators in different countries can compare responses to similar buildings or to detailed aspects of buildings presented as slides or drawings. The value of using this technique is that all investigators are measuring the same response and they all have some confidence that the response they are measuring is an important one, representative of the sort of words and concepts people normally use.

6.4. Testing Hypotheses

There is another way in which the study of underlying dimensions can be of value and this again relates to the fact that the statistical procedure produces dimensions independent of one another. This means that one dimension cannot be thought of as causing the other or indeed as having any relationship to it. We can thus see if one set of attitudes relates to another set by using them both in the same factor analytic procedure. If they both turn out to be highly loaded on different dimensions then we know that they are independent of one another. For instance, if we hypothesise that dissatisfaction with the physical environment is really just part of being dissatisfied with the organisation in general then we can test this hypothesis. To do this we devise a questionnaire containing a variety of questions relating to the physical surroundings and a variety of questions dealing with attitudes towards the organisation.

Table 6.2

Factor loadings for two sets of items as used to test the hypothesis that reactions to the environment and to the organisation are part of the same dimension. The hypothesis is not supported

Summary of questions	Factor loadings* on	
	Factor I	Factor II
Easy to let management know how you feel	−0·80	−0·04
Organisation understands my problems	−0·60	−0·18
Organisation treats employees well	−0·57	−0·25
Do not know what is going on in the organisation	0·46	−0·01
Dissatisfied with day-lighting	0·07	0·78
Dissatisfied with ventilation	0·13	0·56
Satisfied with lighting	−0·26	−0·39
Satisfied with heating	−0·19	−0·34

* These 'loadings' show the degree of relationship between the question and the underlying 'factor' (or dimension). They usually range from $+1·0$ to $−1·0$, the nearer they are to either of these extremes the closer the relationship. In this case values greater than $+$ or $−0·3$ may be taken as indicating a clear relationship to a dimension.

We then factor analyse the responses to this questionnaire and look to see if these two sets of questions are highly loaded on the same dimensions or not. Table 6.2 shows the factor loadings for two such sets of items abstracted from a study with 117 clerical workers (Canter[14]). From this it can be seen quite clearly that the items form two quite independent dimensions and so there is no support for our hypothesis. These are two distinct aspects of job satisfaction.

Besides the interesting implications of this finding in its own right, the process it illustrates for testing hypotheses is a valuable one. Trying to relate two items of a questionnaire to one another is not nearly so valuable an approach as trying to relate two dimensions to one another. The phrasing of any individual item or subtle mis-interpretations of its meaning can produce negative results with one question where a slightly different question on the same topic would produce positive results. The chances of this happening with a number of items is reduced more or less as a direct proportion of the actual number of items used. This is one of the main reasons why psychologists prefer to use sets of items to form standard question-naires rather than the single item of a public opinion poll. They are usually interested in testing hypothesised relationships, but the opinion pollster is interested in establishing descriptive percentage levels for groups in the population.

6.5. Individual Dimensions

So far we have concerned ourselves with the average responses of groups of people but there is no theoretical or practical reason why we shouldn't use the same process with individuals. George Kelly[15] has argued very convincingly that there are many cases in which such individual analyses of dimensions are very valuable. He suggests that there are very big differences between individuals in the type and pattern of dimensions which can be revealed. Kelly's initial concern was with patients undergoing psychotherapy and so it is not surprising that his approach is at the opposite extreme to Osgood's (whose interest was in language in general). Partly because he was concentrating on individuals Kelly also put considerable emphasis on the importance of studying the things described in as much detail as the descriptions. Kelly referred to the descriptions as 'constructs' and the things described as 'elements'. Kelly thus not only concerned himself with the grouping of constructs but also with the way in which the elements were organised. A further development of this was to look at the relationships between the element patterns and those of the constructs. From such analyses a great deal can be learned about an individual's understanding of his world. But because the emphasis is on the individual it has also been considered necessary to use constructs and elements that really are meaningful to him, instead of presenting him with words that he may misunderstand or interpret differently from the investigator. One problem which arises from this when applying it in architecture is that the comparison of people or groups is much easier to do in terms of the structure (*e.g.* many small groupings, or dimensions, or a few large ones) than of the content (*e.g.* houses more like offices than hospitals). This is particularly difficult to deal with when buildings other than private homes are to be considered because a number of people use them and the designer must make some generalisations that at least refer to groups of users if not to the whole population of users.

A compromise is achieved by providing all subjects with the same constructs and elements and analysing these responses separately for each individual, having ensured that the terms used are interpreted in a similar way by all of them. An example of the way such a study works can be provided by comparing the responses of two first year architecture students to the questionnaire shown in Table 6.3. This type of questionnaire, containing a series of constructs and elements selected as particularly relevant to certain individuals or groups, is known as a 'repertory grid'.

To analyse this grid in a way that maintains the richness of the original data, a highly sophisticated computer program developed by Slater[16] was used. The results of this program, however, may be interpreted at a preliminary level with little knowledge of the process. All that is necessary to know is that, like factor analysis, Slater's program organises the elements and constructs of the repertory grid according to a number of dimensions, such that the closer together any two elements or constructs are the more closely related they are in their meaning for, or use by, the individual. Because it has frequently been found that three dimensions explain most of the

Table 6.3
An example of a group repertory grid

Below are a list of places in which you might study. You are to put this list in rank order on *each* of the aspects given

	Your living room at home	Your bedroom at home	Your kitchen at home	Your work table in this school	A table in the library	On a park bench on a sunny day	A study at home	A study in the school (like a staffroom)	An ideal study place
Privacy (Rank 1 for a lot)									
Heating and ventilation (Rank 1 for a lot)									
Control over room (Rank 1 for a lot)									
Distance from lectures (Rank 1 for a little)									
Availability of references (Rank 1 for a lot)									
Amount of distractions (Rank 1 for a little)									
Availability of meals (Rank 1 for easy to get)									
Overall preference (Rank 1 for prefer most)									
Friendliness of environment (Rank 1 for very friendly)									
Adequate furniture (Rank 1 for very adequate)									
Lighting (Rank 1 for good)									
Ease of communication with others (Rank 1 for easy)									

Where do you usually study?..

relationships even with individuals[17] and because three dimensions are easier to comprehend than four or more, Slater takes the major three dimensions and mathematically modifies them so that they will fit on to a sphere. Hence they can be represented in two dimensions by some form of geographical mapping projection. The results of the procedure for two students are shown in Figures 6.1 and 6.2. To understand these figures just remember that they represent points on the surface of a sphere such that the nearer to each other the points are the more 'psychologically' similar they are.

If we look at the centre of Figure 6.1 we will see that having a study in the school comes very close to an 'ideal place to study'. These students actually were provided with desks in an open plan arrangement. We can also see why the school study is so close to the 'ideal' because it is considered to contain all the key attributes such as friendliness, adequate furniture, easier communication with others and little distance from lectures. All of these aspects are about the same distance from the ideal place but some ordering can be achieved by relating them to the construct of overall preference. From this relationship it can be seen that lighting and distance from lectures are the most critical. It is therefore not surprising to learn that this student actually did most of his studying in the school or library, further examination of the figure will show that these are the two places nearest to overall preference. The second student's repertory grid reveals a more intricate pattern. The closest construct to his overall preference is the amount of control he has over the room and secondly, yet some distance from this are privacy, adequate furniture, and possibly ease of communication with others. It is not surprising to learn therefore that a study at home is the nearest to the 'ideal study place' and that in fact this student did the majority of his study in his study bedroom.

This is only a brief analysis of Figures 6.1 and 6.2, but it should be clear that a great deal of detail of both a rich qualitative and precise quantitive kind could be taken from them. This information could be used either for examining the deficiencies in what exists at present or for suggesting future designs. For instance, from a number of student repertory grids it can be seen that having a small study in the school of architecture would only be of value if the student had a lot of control over it.

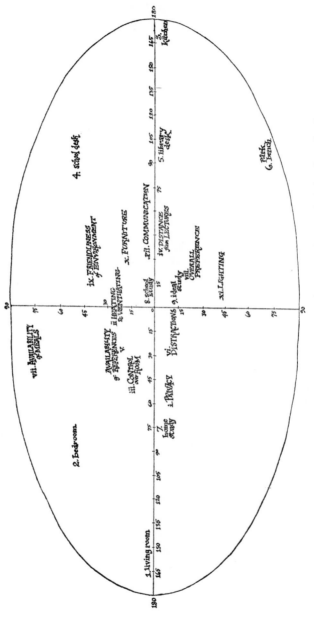

Fig. 6.1. Configuration for a student who worked at a desk in the school.

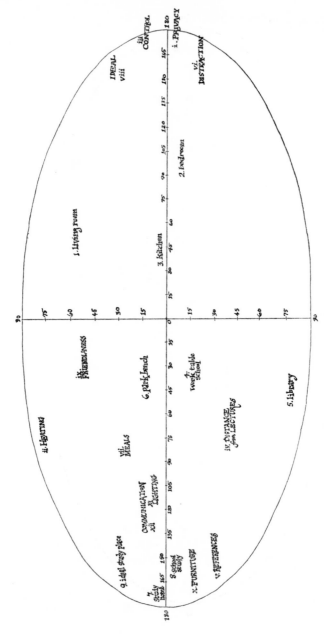

Fig. 6.2.   Configuration for a student who worked at home in a study bedroom.

6.6. Summary and Conclusions

This has been a rather technical chapter. We have been examining methods with little consideration for the theories which gave rise to them. For instance, the various theories of meaning which exist and the particular advantages of the theory put forward by Osgood when he developed the semantic differential have not been discussed. Kelly's personal construct theory out of which the repertory grid has grown is certainly worthy of detailed consideration. However, the methods and results produced by them possibly have, at the present time, wider implications and uses in architecture. This is an unfortunate state of affairs but relates to the fact that there does not appear to be as yet a viable theory which relates people and buildings to one another in the context of design. It is not unlikely that such theories will grow out of questions generated by results of the methods described.

One great value of the discovery of a few underlying dimensions by means of processes such as factor analysis is that it makes practicable the possibility of producing instruments to measure these dimensions and heightens the validity of these instruments. A great deal of research both central and peripheral to architecture has grown out of the development and use of these instruments and it seems as if in the future some of the most important studies will be produced as a direct attack on this approach. Either way an understanding of the concepts and process of finding underlying dimensions will be necessary for future architects.

Another important finding that has been described in this chapter is the difference between the dimensions underlying concepts in general and the dimensions underlying architecture. Whether or not it is also true that architects have, or use, different dimensions from the population at large is still not established although the indications are (e.g. Canter[14]) that the differences are not as great as might be expected. All this means that it should be possible for an architect to communicate with the users of the buildings provided that they ensure they are talking about them in the right way; that they draw upon the central dimensions such as pleasantness and realise that many other comments will only be different ways of referring to this. It seems possible that details of the colour scheme, or the lighting, or the proportion of the spaces are possibly only of as much value as a general indication of whether the building seems to be 'right' or 'wrong', 'good' or 'bad'.

This is not to say that other more detailed information is not possible from the measurement of other aspects of behaviour. In this chapter we have dealt entirely with verbal response. Perhaps this general, relatively unspecific, evaluation of buildings is a characteristic of the way we use words. Perhaps more specific information can be obtained from observations of the way we use space. We shall be examining this in Chapter 8. The further question of the relationship between what we do and what we say is best examined in connection with Reference 18.

One further point we have touched on in this chapter has been the possibility of exploring the differences between individuals. Can we group these differences in some meaningful way? This is the problem we shall be examining in the next chapter.

QUESTIONS FOR DISCUSSION

(1) Looking at the factor loadings below taken from Canter,[14] what dimensions would you say are present?

	Factor loadings		
	I	II	III
Uninteresting–interesting	−0·51	−0·21	+0·27
Unstable–stable	−0·19	−0·60	−0·04
Dirty–clean	−0·23	−0·60	+0·04
Passive–active	−0·27	−0·15	+0·62
Sad–happy	−0·67	−0·36	+0·24
Unpleasant–pleasant	−0·68	−0·42	+0·09
Slow–fast	−0·14	−0·14	+0·61
Calm–lively	−0·01	−0·00	+0·75
Discordant–harmonious	−0·30	−0·74	+0·09

(2) What types of dimensions are likely to occur if you were to factor analyse a repertory grid in the normal way (*i.e.* treating each *cell* as a separate variable)? An example of precisely this is given in Canter.[6]

(3) In what ways do underlying dimensions do an injustice to everyday experience?

(4) It has been suggested that factor analysis is like getting the data in a stranglehold around the neck and saying 'speak to me!' What do you think?

Chapter 7

Individual Differences

7.1. A Lay Attack

One of the strongest arguments which laymen feel they can bring to bear against the possibility of a scientific psychology is that everyone is different. It is maintained that even if general laws for average behaviour could be found there would still be so much individual variation that these laws could be of little practical value in explaining or predicting our experiences of other people in daily life. With relation to buildings, in particular, it is thought that people differ from one another so much in relation to their reactions that this would make it impossible to identify clear trends.

There are two answers to this argument. The first is the empirical one that consistencies in behaviour have been observed both between identifiable groups and within them. The second is that it is precisely the occurrence of individual variation which has stimulated much of psychological research. For if we can identify the ways in which people differ from each other and the phenomena which give rise to these differences we will have a fuller understanding of human behaviour in general.

7.2. The New Machiavellianism

One way in which people seem to differ is in their ability or preparedness to manipulate or make use of others. In the sixteenth century a Florentine, Machiavelli, wrote a series of essays discussing in some detail the tactics available to politicians for manipulating people to their own advantage. In the late 1950s an American psychologist, Christie,[1] considered the possibility that people who agreed in general terms with Machiavelli would be predictably different in a variety of aspects of their behaviour from those who disagreed. To examine this he selected a large number of statements from the essays of Machiavelli and processed them (in a similar way to those discussed in Chapter 6) to find those most closely related to the central theme of the essays. This provided him with a standardised questionnaire; that is a series of statements to present to people in order to ask for their degree of agreement or disagreement. These were such items as: 'The best way to handle people is to tell them what they want to hear', 'Anyone who completely trusts anyone else is asking for trouble' and 'It is wise to flatter important people'.

Because of the emphasis in the writings of Machiavelli on the manipulation of others, one crucial test of whether the answers to these items is actually providing a valid measure of the ways in which people differ from one another is to relate these answers to actual behaviour in an interpersonal bargaining situation. One such test of validity was to have groups of three subjects agree amongst themselves on the way they would split $10 between them, given the condition that only two of the three were allowed to benefit from the division. Only seven groups of three were put through this 'game' but the results are revealing. People with high Machiavellianism scores obtained on average $5.57, those with middle scores $3.14 and those with low scores only averaged $1.29.

This is a good example of the approach of psychologists to the study of individual differences. However, the Machiavellianism scale has also been mentioned because it is a plausible hypothesis that it is an important variable in determining success as an architect. It raises the further issue of whether those who attempt to manipulate others are also more likely to manipulate the non-human aspects of their environment.

In general, psychologists have not concerned themselves with the latter problem, being more interested in the interpersonal aspect of individual differences. The degree to which the dimensions of individual differences isolated by psychologists will help to explain variations in reactions to the physical environment remains to be demonstrated.

However, on an *a priori* basis it does seem that there are certain established differences between people which may well have implications for the understanding of the interaction between people and their environment. This chapter will summarise some of those distinctions which, on the face of it at least, may be expected to prove fruitful in the future.

7.3. The Study of Individual Differences

In general, there have been two approaches to the study of individual differences. On the one hand people have developed a theory of the mechanisms which control human behaviour and have shown how it is that these mechanisms do in turn give rise to differences between people. The Freudian approach to personality is one which typifies this. On the other hand, dimensions of individual differences have been found from analyses (like those described in Chapter 6) of a wide range of responses. In some cases, these responses have been mainly answers to questionnaire items but there are cases in which they have related to other behavioural measurements. The work of Eysenck is an example of this latter approach, although like most of the other researchers in the field, once the various dimensions of individual variation have been established, an attempt is made to generate a theory which will explain the mechanisms which give rise to this differentiation. The example of Machiavellianism does to some degree combine these two approaches, moving as it does from a philosophical definition to measurements of behavioural response. But this is somewhat unusual in that neither the basic psychological mechanisms nor the pool of behaviours from which the dimension has been drawn are clarified. The studies of Machiavellianism do show, however, that it is possible to make progress by developing measurements specifically related to particular areas of interest. It is worth bearing in mind that this might be the most productive approach in the architectural context, rather than attempting to use measurements already in existence within psychology. These existing measures may not necessarily be of relevance to the problems with which architects are confronted.

7.4. Age, Sex and Class

Apart from these two approaches to the clarification of individual differences, there is a third approach which draws more heavily upon the common sense understanding of personal variation. It is clearly the case that knowledge of whether a person is male or female, old or young, or of a high social status or a low social status, will enable us to predict a lot about their behaviour. However, one difficulty with using these sorts of variables is that they often summarise a complex set of psychological phenomena and, as a consequence, do not enable us to explain much of the behaviour they help to predict. For instance, older people, besides having different physiological reactions to young people, also tend to have had different job experiences, have been brought up in a culture with different attitudes and are, at the time of study, often in a different social situation from younger people. So although it is useful to think in terms of old as opposed to young respondents (for example in order to predict which people are more likely to be able to find their way around a new building), this will not necessarily allow us to specify the reasons for different behaviours to the degree that is necessary if we are to modify designs in a meaningful way, although our study of development in Chapter 5 does show ways in which our knowledge of a person's age can be of use.

Similarly, sex differences are often confounded with differences in family role, job types, training and experience as well as the more obvious physiological and anatomical distinctions. None the less, in the great majority of psychological situations it is found that men perform differently from women. In her commendably readable book Hutt[2] summarises the differences between males and females thus: 'the male is physically stronger but less resilient, he is more independent, adventurous and aggressive, he is more ambitious and competitive, he has greater spatial, numerical and mathematical ability, he is more likely to construe the world in terms of objectives, ideas and theories. The female at the outset possesses those sensory capabilities which facilitate inter-personal communion; physically and psychologically she matures more rapidly, her verbal skills are precocious and fluent, she is more nurturent, affiliative, more consistent, and is likely to construe the world in personal, moral and aesthetic terms'. As Hutt emphasises there is a great overlap between the sexes so that there is a reasonable probability of finding males with the female characteristics listed above and vice versa. However, the fact that such profound differences run through such a large number and wide range of human behaviours does imply that in any situation in which we are interested in individual variation, it will be necessary to take sex differences into account. This applies both at

the practical level in which we may be considering the design of
buildings for different types of personnel and at the theoretical level
when we are trying to explain human behaviour in relation to other
characteristics. Thus dimensions of personality like those with which
we shall be concerning ourselves later, often show a marked tendency
to relate to sex differences.

As Bromley[3] has shown in some detail, age differences are almost
as broad in their influence as those of sex. The implications of this
are not apparent within general psychology because some of the
most available groups of subjects for psychologists are often either
university undergraduates or school children, and so we are still in
some doubt about the general changes which take place once people
have left those institutions in which senior personnel are engaged in
psychological research!

Social class is, of course, a central variable in sociology and so
there is a considerable literature on the differences between the
behaviour of people in the different classes (*e.g.* Reference 4). These
differences have psychological as well as sociological implications,
both because the experience and attitudes of people in different
classes is demonstrably different and because the variables of age and
sex, which we have already briefly considered, do also inter-relate
with the one of social class.

Age, sex and social class, then, cannot be dismissed when
considering people's reactions to buildings because it is almost
certain that in the great majority of cases these variables will reveal
significant differences in reactions. However, the relative impurity of
any one of these variables, its complexity and lack of specificity,
does mean that it is necessary to proceed further if we are to get a
full understanding of what it is that gives rise to individual variation
in response.

7.5. Field Dependence

There has been one series of psychological studies of individual
differences which has concentrated upon an individual's ability to
distinguish stimuli from the context in which they are presented.
This work, associated with the name of Witkin *et al.*[5] gained its

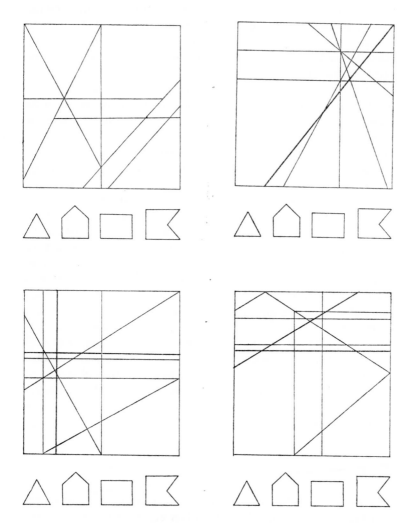

Fig. 7.1.   An example of an embedded figures test. (Instruction: circle that simple figure which is hidden in the complex one above it.)

impetus from perceptual studies in which a person in a darkened room, presented with a luminous rod within a square luminous frame, rotated the rod until it appeared to be vertical. Various confusions were introduced in order to make this task more difficult. The two basic manipulations were first to rotate the luminous frame so that it was not aligned vertically and the second was to tip the seat in which the subject was sitting so that it was also not at a vertical angle. The degree to which these confusions do produce errors in the perception of verticality may be thought of as an indication of the degree to which a subject is influenced by the context or field; subjects being greatly influenced, being referred to as field dependent. Reference to Chapter 3 in which we looked at Gestalt psychology will show that this approach owes much to those formulations.

As shown in the example of Machiavellianism earlier, one test of the value of a measure of individual variation is the number of other aspects of behaviour to which it can be related. In the case of psychological differentiation it seems that although field dependence is to some degree related to general intelligence, there are a number of aspects of behaviour which it helps to clarify. It does, for instance, relate to the ability to find simple figures embedded in more complex ones, the sort of task often found in children's comics and illustrated in Figure 7.1. It also relates to certain aspects of creativity, in particular to originality as shown, for instance, by the number of uses which can be thought of for various household objects. All this leads to the suggestion that a person's ability to differentiate objects from their surroundings might well be an important personality characteristic, one which it seems possible would relate to a person's interaction with buildings.

7.6. Cognitive Complexity

Instead of dealing with perceptual phenomena it can be shown that another way in which people differ consistently relates to the structure of aspects of their cognition.

In this case individuals are distinguished not in terms of their place along some common continua, such as Machiavellianism or field dependence, but in terms of the number of dimensions they themselves have for construing people (or sometimes things) and the relationships between those dimensions. For instance, one architect may think of buildings almost entirely in terms of the proportions of their facades whilst another may think of them in terms only of their cost per square foot. Both these people are similar in that they each look at buildings from a single viewpoint. They would be different from others who thought about buildings from many different viewpoints. These differences relate to their cognition and its underlying patterns or 'structure'. The former, with a single dimension, have a 'simple' structure when compared with the latter who are 'cognitively complex'.

This distinction owes much to communication and information theory as it draws an analogy between different types of communication channel. Some channels can carry a wide range of different types of information whereas others are very limited in what they can support. Other distinctions can be made between those which can carry a lot and those which can carry a little information. The application of these analogies depends upon the type of measurement technique used and, as a consequence, there has grown up a great variety of definitions and measures of cognitive complexity each of which is not necessarily measuring the same thing as all the others.

Indeed there is a discussion amongst psychologists in this field as to whether cognitive complexity is a central feature of each individual relating to all the things about which he thinks, or whether it is necessary to talk about cognitive complexity with regard to a particular set of phenomena, for any given person. The evidence[6,7] tends to favour the latter viewpoint. From everyday experience it is apparent that a person who can consider, say, wines from a great number of viewpoints, is not necessarily able to bring as great a range of orientations to bear when considering dogs.

The potentials of the cognitive complexity aspect of personality for the understanding of the reactions of people to buildings as well as for clarifying differences in the approach of designers are many (*see* for example, Reference 8). But one of the main possibilities for its future application is that, theoretically at least, it may be considered as one important aspect of 'expertise' or 'sophistication' with regard to any particular set of stimuli. The idea behind this can be easily appreciated by considering any 'expert'. What distinguishes him from the non-expert with regard to the judgements he makes in his area of expertise? One of the more obvious distinctions is that he is aware of a far greater number of possible differences between things and that he can, or at least is prepared to, differentiate more precisely between degrees of these differences than the non-expert. This thus provides us with possible ways of measuring that expertise and thus of relating it to other activities.

For instance it might be expected that architecture students who were more complex in their judgements of buildings would do better in their courses than others. In a small study to test this[9] it was found to be the case. Another aspect of complexity indicated by the studies of Bieri *et al.*[10] is that the more complex person is more likely to be consistent in the view he holds and is more able to deal with conflicting information.

The structural analogy may be likened to the difference between the complex 'geodesic dome' and the simple 'lean-to'. In the former small changes in the environment or even in the structure itself will have little effect on the building in general, whereas in the latter one strut removed or changed can cause the structure to collapse. Little is known about the complexity of users with regard to buildings but there are indications (mainly from common experience) that people are more complex about other people than they ever are about buildings. This suggests that the effects of buildings upon the perception of others might have a much greater impact than upon the direct perception of buildings themselves.

7.7. *Extraversion and Neuroticism*

In the past 20 years, H. J. Eysenck and his collaborators have poured out a vast literature around the personality dimensions of extraversion and neuroticism (*e.g.* References 11 and 12). Thus whilst no survey, however brief, of the personality literature would be complete without some reference to this area, the possibility of summarising it is clearly difficult even for Eysenck himself who is at present publishing at the rate of at least three books a year.

The distinctions Eysenck draws revolve around a self-report questionnaire but none the less also relate to such different psychological theorists as Jung and Pavlov. The questionnaire, which has gone through a number of forms, consists of items which have been shown by factor analysis to produce two dimensions which have been called the degree of extraversion and the degree of neuroticism of the respondent.

These dimensions have now crept into popular understanding but as a consequence have lost some of their original precision. It must not be forgotten that the basic dimensions do relate to responses given on questionnaire items and that it is, in effect, the group of questionnaire items which defines the dimension. Thus for clarification of the dimension we must always relate back to the particular items used.

Extraversion is seen as having its opposite in introversion and although these two ideas do relate to the person's interests in things outside of himself it is tempting for architects to see an immediate relationship to being influenced by the environment or not influenced. The details of the studies show that this is far too simple a description. Besides the fact that we must always remember that we are talking about a person's position along an underlying continuum and are not classifying people into one type or the other, it is also clear from analysis of the questions that extraversion has two distinct sub-groups. These relate to the concepts of sociability, the interest in and awareness of other people, gaining enjoyment from parties rather than from books, etc., and another component of impulsivity. The term for this latter aspect expresses it quite aptly, indicating as it does the degree to which a person will act on impulse rather than after detailed, careful consideration.

Neuroticism has its alternative pole in the concept of normality and is often described as the degree to which a person is emotionally labile. In other words, the degree to which he responds to situations in an emotional way. At the extreme, this leads to the whole range of behaviours which are commonly thought of as neurotic, particularly with regard to worrying about the situation in which the person finds himself or his ability to cope.

In recent years Eysenck and his collaborators have developed an explanation of the mechanisms underlying these differences in people which has its roots in the physiological hypothesis of arousal. Expressed briefly, this suggests that there is a curvilinear relationship between the level of emotional arousal and the efficiency or effectiveness of psychological performance such as that shown in Figure 7.2. The idea behind this relationship, first formulated by Yerkes and Dodson[13] is simply expressed by pointing out that when we are very drowsy or indeed asleep, our performance is very ineffective and inefficient and when we are so stimulated that we are what is often referred to in lay terms as 'over excited', we also do not perform very well. There seems to be some sort of optimum level of psychological arousal at which we perform best.

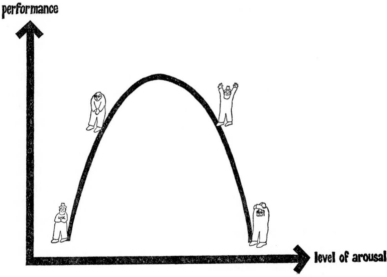

Fig. 7.2.   The arousal hypothesis and individual differences.

The idea behind Eysenck's explanation of personality is that each individual has his own built-in levels of arousal or arousability and thus each person starts at a different level along this curve. Thus those high in extraversion being at a lower level require more stimulation to reach their optimum, whereas those high in introversion require less stimulation (particularly social stimulation) to reach the same optimum level. It would require some detailed analysis of the nature of the hypothesised physiological mechanisms of arousal to draw out the implications of all these theories for the explanation of the established differences in personality, but most explanations revolve around the idea that there are different mechanisms of arousal for each of the dimensions of personality isolated (*see* for instance, Claridge[14]).

Some studies have shown that those high in extraversion are more likely to learn a task which produces an increase in stimulation, whereas those high in introversion are more likely to learn a task which reduces the amount of stimulation.[15] It therefore seems plausible that more general relationships between these dimensions and aspects of the physical surroundings may eventually be established. Hill[16] did find some indication that there was a relationship between the amount of privacy people selected and their position on the extraversion dimension but other unpublished studies have in fact produced opposite results. As can be seen from the curvilinear relationship presented in Figure 7.2, small differences in the amount of stimulation involved may produce seemingly conflicting results. Thus for this theory to be productive, it is necessary to specify the conditions of stimulation in great detail. It also is possible that different types of stimulation will have quite different effects.

Within this context it is worth noting (in relation to Chapter 3) that Berlyne[17] has argued in some detail the case for most aesthetic responses being related to the ideas of optimum levels of arousal, and while he worked mainly with simple aesthetic phenomena some researchers (Kuller[18]) are now beginning to look at the possibilities of similar results using stimuli which come directly from architecture.

7.8. Creativity and Intelligence

Whilst we are considering differences between people it is important to draw attention to an area of differences in which psychologists have carried out many and various studies. These are the areas which generally relate to what is called intellectual ability. Intelligence tests now form a large part of the contemporary educational vocabulary and there is no indication that their number is being reduced. In general terms these tests have been developed in much the same way as measures of personality and have been developed so that they measure the different dimensions of intellectual ability which have been established. A general underlying dimension of overall intelligence seems to characterise most of these tests and beyond that tests which deal with verbal, spatial and numerical aspects have been developed. These tests measure the degree to which a person is able to cope with intellectual problems and as such have been shown to relate to a wide range of achievements in later life. It seems clear that a certain level of achievement in any intelligence test is necessary if a person is to benefit from higher education, but over recent years, one of the major criticisms of these tests has been that they only deal with a person's ability to resolve problems which have a specific solution, which lead to a 'convergent answer'. As a consequence, there has been an attempt to develop measures relating to what is loosely called creativity, that is, problems which do not have one specific solution but require 'divergent thinking'. The difficulty with these latter tests is that, almost by definition, they are difficult to score in a truly objective way and as a consequence those aspects of creativity such as fluency (or number of responses), originality (or frequency of producing responses different from those produced by others) and other scoring methods relating to a classification of the actual responses produced have been developed.

The relevance for architects, of dividing up people according to intellectual ability are at two levels. At the level of the users of buildings it would seem that people with different intellectual abilities would be able to cope or would be likely to deal with the building in different ways and, as a consequence, it would be necessary to take these different patterns of behaviour into account. This is especially the case for buildings normally housing groups from different ranges of the population. At a more fundamental level, it should be realised that public buildings may well be used by people drawn from the lowest as well as the highest range of intellectual level. On the other hand, from the point of view of understanding the design process, it is clear that we must take the intellectual capabilities of different designers into account and to understand the ways in which these different abilities give rise to different types of buildings.

7.9. Conclusions

We have examined briefly a wide range of ways in which people may differ and seen that in all of them there are possible implications for the use and design of the physical environment. However, it seems likely that for some time to come the most important contribution of this area of psychology to design will be the awareness it gives to the designer of the fact that people do differ, and an indication of the ways in which they differ. He can then consider a broad range of potential users and behaviours in his building and not make the common assumption that most people are similar to himself.

QUESTIONS FOR DISCUSSION

(1) Would you try to cope with differences in the intelligence of building users when designing an office block? How?

(2) What differences between building users do you consider it important for architects to take into account?

(3) What differences between architects do you consider it important for building users to take into account?

(4) Should there be any relationship between the answers to Questions 2 and 3? In what situations?

(5) Which personality dimension would you expect to relate to preference for room size, extraversion, field dependence, Machiavellianism? How would you test these expectancies? How would you apply the results?

Chapter 8

The Use of Space

8.1. Territorial Behaviour

If you were to spend some time in the New England spruce woods watching the activities of the Myrtle, Cape May and black-throated green species of warbler, you would probably notice that although they shared similar trees they tended to be found in different parts of those trees.[1] The Myrtle warblers are most commonly located in the lower part of the trees, the Cape May warblers at the top and the black-throated green warblers at the bottom. These differences of habitat have the interesting effect of reducing the competition for food which might otherwise occur between the species.

Within a given species, too, distinct patterns of distribution over space can be observed. Grazing cattle and sea birds when resting or feeding both tend to spread themselves out evenly over the area the herd or flock is occupying. Like the New England warblers these animals are reducing competition amongst themselves by the judicious (indeed socialistic) use of the space and, hence, food resources available to them.

Adaptation to the physical environment and the resources provided by it is an important aspect of survival. It is therefore not surprising that mechanisms for efficient interaction with the environment should have evolved in a way that is equally beneficial to a number of different species. These mechanisms include a great variety of ways of ensuring that the habitat to which a species is most suited is not used by, or in some cases even is not available to, those other species who are the most likely competitors, due, for instance, to their feeding, mating or nesting habits.

There are situations in which the physical characteristics of the species are not sufficient to lead to the differentiation of habitats for species, or areas for individuals. In these cases social mechanisms often develop which have the same biological effect, that of increasing the efficiency of use of natural resources, the maintenance of

108

mating behaviour and so on. These social mechanisms usually take the form of defence of specific areas or 'territory'. This 'territoriality' takes many forms. As Klopfer[2] illustrates, although the basic notion is the defence of a particular area against intruders of the same species and sex, many examples can be found of defence against members of different species, or defence by a group of a communal territory. The boundaries of the territory may be small and clearly defined, or large, intricate and diffuse. They may change with the seasons or the stages in the life cycle of the animal.

Territoriality is thus an aspect of the social organisation of animals that is an adaptation, but it is important to remember that it is in the nature of such adaptations to vary from species to species and environment to environment, otherwise their adaptive function would be very weak indeed. The realisation of the variety of territorial behaviour in animals is particularly important when we try to make extrapolations from it to human beings. For as we saw in Chapter 4 every person has a great potential for adapting to his environment through the process of learning. People are not as dependent upon inherited physical characteristics or patterns of behaviour as other animals are because they can, during their early years, and in later day to day activities, learn how to cope with developments and changes in their social and physical surroundings.

One important result of this capacity to learn is the rapid development of behaviour patterns from generation to generation and even within generations, one of the most notable outcomes of this being the development of speech. This ability to deal with conceptual representations without the actual presence of an object or a situation increases enormously man's power to cope with his environment. Speech then, and the power to learn associations by means of it, requires a totally different orientation towards that behaviour in man which might seem superficially to be analogous to territorial behaviour in animals. Indeed as Hediger,[3] one of the leaders in the study of territorial behaviour in animals, has pointed out, territoriality in animals can be thought of as acting as a speech saving device. Because animals do organise themselves in territorial groups there is less need for them to communicate with one another about such essentials as the location of food, the movement of predators or the need for a mate. It could thus be argued that as man developed speech so the patterns of his spatially related activities diverged from those of the other animals to which he was related.

This point has been emphasised because it is all too easy to make a simple extrapolation from the behaviour of animals to that of man. These extrapolations are often very inviting to the lay reader because they can often take the form of a dramatic analogy which captures the imagination but in so doing ignores (or glosses over) those qualities of human behaviour which make it uniquely human.

There are many ways in which human beings make use of space, and a careful examination of these uses does show that something other than obvious functional requirements influences them. At the end of this chapter we shall briefly examine some of the theories which have been put forward to suggest what these other influences are, but in order that the reader can judge for himself without pre-judice we shall first look at observations of the way people use space.

8.2. Location in Space

Even casual observation of people in public waiting areas reveals that they do not spread themselves out evenly across the space available. Neither do they necessarily wait in that place which is functionally most appropriate. Stilitz[4] observed people waiting in London Underground stations and theatre foyers and found that they tended to wait out of the line of the traffic flow near to pillars. In Japan, Kamino[5] carried out similar studies in railway stations. Figure 8.1 is drawn from his results. There also it can be seen that people tend to locate themselves near pillars but out of the line of the flow of traffic. Both Stilitz and Kamino came to the conclusion that people were trying to position themselves in a place from which they could see but in which they were not too obvious or too much in the way of people moving. It also seems likely that the pillars provided something against which to lean in the absence of seats.

Groups of individuals can also be observed to locate themselves in space according to clear patterns. Figure 8.2 shows one of the clearest of these patterns, people sitting in restaurants. From this figure it can be seen that people tend to sit at the tables around the periphery of the restaurant rather than those at the middle. In some restaurants this is such a frequently occurring pattern that the

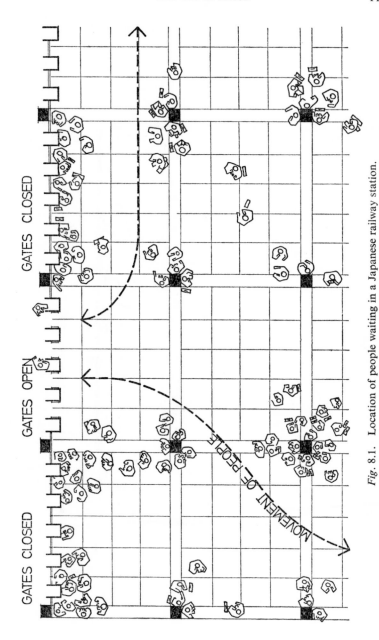

Fig. 8.1. Location of people waiting in a Japanese railway station.

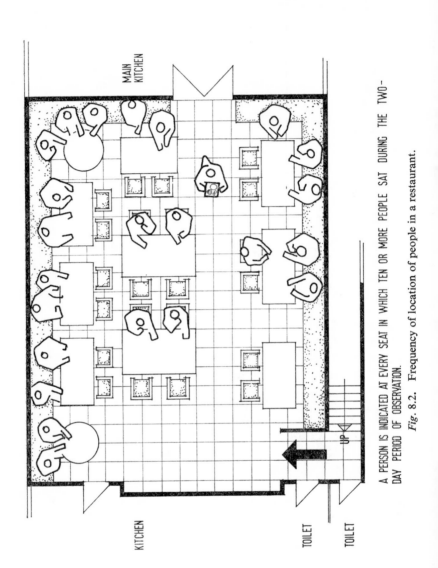

Fig. 8.2. Frequency of location of people in a restaurant.

A PERSON IS INDICATED AT EVERY SEAT IN WHICH TEN OR MORE PEOPLE SAT DURING THE TWO-DAY PERIOD OF OBSERVATION.

tables with which the waiters have to deal are divided according to this pattern, and because the amount of gratuities a waiter may receive relates to the number of customers he serves the more senior waiters deal with the peripheral tables and the 'new boy' is given the central tables.

Beyond these observations of people in public places relatively little study has been carried out of the way in which people relate themselves to physical objects in a wide range of situations. This is a pity because it is clear that people do not make use of their physical surroundings in a random way. Indeed much of architecture assumes that quite definite patterns will occur. For instance, it is often assumed that a particular furniture arrangement will be used in rooms and they are designed with this in mind. Many architects are surprised to find that the arrangements which seem obvious to them do not actually occur.

One reason why so little study has been made of the relationships which people take up *vis-à-vis* their *physical* surroundings is the observation that much of human spatial behaviour is more readily explained in terms of the relationships people take up in respect to other *people*. The observations of waiting behaviour or of seat selection in a restaurant could well be re-interpreted in terms of people using the physical environment to enable them to locate themselves in a desired position with respect to the activities of others rather than simply their physical surroundings. However, it must not be forgotten that there clearly are cases in which people do deal with physical entities seemingly independently of their social implications. One example that I have noted frequently is the fact that people waiting near bus stops in Glasgow tend to stand slightly further away from the bus stop itself than they do from one another. Informal observations suggest that while the mean distance between people is a little over two feet the mean distance people stand from the bus stop is nearer to three feet. Perhaps the reader can think of other examples of more importance to designers.

8.3. *Interpersonal Distance*

As described above, many animals can be observed to spread themselves out evenly when they are feeding so that the distance they maintain from one another is more or less the same. In situations where people have little opportunity for any other way of behaving, such as on a crowded beach, similar behaviour can be observed. The space which people in such situations seem to be keeping between themselves, the space below which they feel what might be described as an invasion of privacy, is often referred to as 'personal space'.

Hall[6] taking an anthropological approach has put forward many suggestions about the nature of this 'hidden dimension' which keeps people at set distances from one another, and Sommer[7] has carried out a number of psychological studies which explore this. One thing which emerges from both the work of Hall and Sommer is that 'personal space' is not a simple unitary concept in which the individual can be considered the centre of a symmetrical bubble. The most elementary observations show that this distance varies from group to group or from situation to situation. Observations we carried out on people waiting for buses in Edinburgh showed that men stood further away from other people than women did but that both men and women stood further away from people of the opposite sex than from people of the same sex. Leibman[8] showed that the position in which women decided to sit was influenced by the race and sex of another person nearby. In a situation in which subjects were asked to arrange 'actors' at different distances from one another, Little[9] found that they were placed at different distances depending on whether they were in an office, lobby, campus or street. They were also placed at different distances depending on whether they were friends, acquaintances or strangers.

However, in certain clearly defined situations constant inter-personal distances can be observed. In an elegant study Sommer[7] asked pairs of subjects to sit in the best place for informal conversation. They were provided with two couches facing each other and so they could decide to sit opposite each other or side by side. The distance between the couches was varied in order to find whether there was one distance beyond or below which people preferred to sit side by side. In other words an optimum seating distance for this situation was identified. Sommer found that this was about 3 feet 6 inches. I repeated the experiment recently with students who knew nothing of Sommer's work and obtained a distance of 3 feet 2 inches. Considering the room for error in the measurements, these distances may be considered to be the same, showing a remarkable consistency over time and place in the results.

Exploring the situation of informal conversation a stage further Sommer examined the preference for sitting opposite or side by side when having an informal conversation. He found a clear preference for face to face seating except when the face to face distance was greater than that when seated side by side. My own study corroborated this. In fact in a small study I carried out in Japan with young female students, I found it virtually impossible to get them to sit next to the target person. In some cases they preferred to sit opposite him even if the only available seat was 12 feet away. I remain unconvinced that the fact that *I* was the target person had any major bearing on these results!

Research which throws light on these interpersonal distances in conversation is that by Argyle[10] and his colleagues. They have dis-covered a number of aspects of behaviour that seem to play an important part in ensuring that a conversation flows smoothly. In particular they have isolated head movement and the mutual eye contact associated with it as being important in controlling the mood and tempo of a conversation between two people. This suggests that distance has an effect on the way a conversation might proceed possibly within quite narrow limits. Some corroboration for this comes from a study in Japan by Oyama (personal communica-tion) in which he found that certain parts of Japanese speech, particularly those related to the mood of the conversation, occurred with different frequency when the two people were at different distances.

If eye contact and head movements do influence interaction it might be expected that the angle of the two people from one another was important. We have already seen that in some situations a face to face arrangement is preferred but there is a considerable amount of other evidence to show that angle influences the distance which people prefer to be from one another. One study[11] showed that angle also has an effect on the distance groups of students prefer to place themselves from a lecturer. In that study students were asked, in groups of eight, to go into a seminar room in order to take part in an experiment. On entering the room they found a lecturer who gave them a questionnaire and asked them to sit down. He then noted the seats in which they sat. Two things were varied for different groups of subjects, the distance the lecturer stood from the front row and the arrangement of the furniture either in straight lines or in a semi-circle. When the lecturer stood about ten feet away from the front row the students tended to sit in the first three rows of seats. When he stood about one and a half feet from the front row they sat in the last three rows. In the semi-circular arrangement there was no difference between the two positions of the lecturer. It therefore appears that the arrangement of the furniture and the increased variation in angle which the semi-circular arrangement provides counteracts the distance preferences indicated in the rectangular arrangement.

A further development of the effects of angle is shown by Sommer's studies of interaction at tables. Using both field experiments in which people were observed sitting in different places and surveys in which people were asked to indicate the arrangements most suitable for different activity, Sommer has been able to show that the type of interaction which people have is best suited by different seating arrangements. With a rectangular table he found that for conversation the most preferred position was at either side of a corner. On the other hand when two people are competing with one another they prefer to be face to face across the long side of the table. In situations in which they are co-operating sitting side by side seems to be most preferable and when they are just co-acting, not requiring any interaction with one another, then they prefer to be at opposite corners facing one another. It might well be expected that there are big cultural differences in these arrangements, but in a small study which I was able to carry out in Japan I found substantially similar results to those of Sommer. The only difference was that when the Japanese subjects were given instructions for a competitive situation they still sat next to one another. This was possibly due to the fact that they did not really compete in the western sense but rather co-operated in the way that they would produce differing results.

The implications of these arrangements when the two people were strangers to one another was also explored by Sommer both by using stooges in a library and by observing the order in which seats were taken up at library tables. He found that in all cases an attempt was made to sit as far as possible away from the person already sitting at the table and when distance was reduced to use a side position which thus reduced the possibility for eye contact.

So far we have only looked at the work which examines the taking up of static positions, in which interaction is at a minimum, but even in these cases we have seen that the positions taken seem to be related to the type or quality of interaction which might be expected in those seating arrangements. It would therefore be expected that observations of activity would reveal differences related to the position in which people were. Observing the amount of participation in classrooms Sommer reports a decrease as the seating position moves towards the sides and towards the back of the room. This can be seen as a direct counterpart of the seat selected to reduce interaction, showing once again that a general pattern relating interpersonal distance to social interaction can be observed. One area in which this relationship can be found to be quite specific is in the leadership of a group. It is commonly accepted that the chairman of a committee sits at the head of a table and Sommer[12] has shown that even in informal situations the person who does most talking or who dominates the group in other ways tends also to sit at the end of the table. In informal situations, whether or not the leader emerges because he is the person who sits at the head of the table, or that the person who leads will tend to try to sit in that position, has so far not been determined. It seems likely that both possibilities occur.

In a most interesting study De Long[13] showed that the details of a group organisation could be read from the positions of people around a table. He made notes of the seating taken up by people during the course of a series of seminars. At one point in the seminars a student took over the leadership from the professor. Ratings of the support given to the professor and the student leader showed a clear relationship to the distance of that person's seat from the two people. The two people sat at either end of the table and it was found that support was highest at the seat to the right of them and decreased along the length of the table.

We can now begin to see why there is such concern and discussion about the shapes of tables at international committees and why at one stage in the Paris peace talks about the Vietnam war there was much heated discussion, and for a time deadlock, over whether the table around which the talks should take place should be round or square. The shape of the table and the positions in which people sit may have major implications for the way in which interactions take place.

8.4. Human Territoriality

We have moved quite a long way from our first discussion on the habits of the New England warblers and we have seen that the evidence from empirical studies is very difficult to cast in the mould of animal behaviour. It is possible to think of personal space in animals as being a physical space which is carried around with them keeping others at constant distances, but even with animals we have seen that these distances can vary considerably from situation to situation. When we deal with human beings it is not really possible to think of this space in physical analogies (such as a bubble) but rather as a way in which people use space in various interactions.

In the animal world a distinction is made between personal space, the distance animals keep from one another, and territory which is the area they defend. For people Hall[6] suggests that there are four major distances at which they interact, that for intimate friends, that for casual friends, that for social-consultative encounters and that for other acquaintances. There is little detailed empirical evidence for these variations but the general idea commends itself for further study. The meaning of human territory and territorial behaviour beyond these interpersonal distances is much more problematic. It is only in the extreme situations of war or gang fights that defence of territories can be seen to be a major motivating force for human behaviour. In most other situations quite distinct functional requirements can be brought to bear to explain why people keep others out of a given area. It is not necessary to draw upon some innate instinct for the defence of territory, to explain why people want to work in a room on their own. The chances of them maintaining peace, quiet and privacy are greatly increased if they keep the room to themselves. Similarly in a capital oriented society defence of property against intruders is the obvious functional thing to do. So although, as with personal space, it is useful to take the concept of territoriality from the animal kingdom and examine its relevance to human beings, we must realise that the concept changes considerably when applied to people. Indeed it loses much of its inevitable or mystical quality. Instead it becomes a summary of a series of pieces of human behaviour which can be observed to occur in particular situations.

It is clear that in certain cases, particularly where communication between people is critical or difficult, behaviour analogous to animal territoriality can be observed. Amongst old people, for instance, Lipman[14] in Britain and Araki[15] in Japan have shown that preferred chairs or areas of the room were defended against intruders to the point of physical violence. In many houses also, the head of the family may have a seat which is defended against others. In this case we can already see that it is the implications of possessing that seat and the status it assumes that are important.

Territoriality may well be an important concept in understanding human spatial behaviour but unfortunately the current discussion of this concept has been so befuddled that it is difficult to evaluate exactly what it means. I prefer to deal either with functional requirements associated with specific use of a particular area or with the implications of preferences for a particular position.

One series of studies which has contributed to our understanding of consistent preferences for particular seats or sides of the table has been that by Altman.[16] He studied pairs of people who were confined together in one space. The people, who were members of the American Navy, were supposed to stay in their confined situation for eight days but many of them insisted on being released before that time—they 'aborted'. Altman found that one of the key differences between the groups which aborted and the groups which did not was the degree to which they showed, early in their confinement, consistent preferences for particular sides of the room, table and chairs. Those which did not abort showed a much greater amount of 'territorial' behaviour than those which did, thus suggesting that in this rather unusual situation these consistent preferences were either a counterpart of, or led to, compatible social interaction.

8.5. Patterns of Communication in Space

Before we try to summarise the general theory and architectural implications which arise from these studies, it is valuable to consider

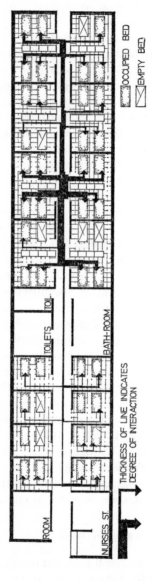

Fig. 8.3.   Friendship patterns in a hospital.

one other series of studies. This shows the relationships between patterns of human behaviour and the architectural configurations within which that behaviour takes place.

One of the earliest of these studies was that by Festinger *et al.*[17] They examined the patterns of friendships which occurred in different housing layouts using a method known as sociometry developed by Moreno.[18] Sociometry consists of asking of each individual with whom he is friendly (friendliness may be defined either by reference to actions such as going shopping together, or simply as degree of acquaintance). From the responses to this question friendship patterns can be drawn up and individuals who have many friends or who have few friends can be identified. Festinger *et al.* found that those people more centrally placed in the housing layouts had more friends. These studies have been repeated in offices, classrooms and other places,[19-21] but possibly the largest series of studies has been carried out by Kurihara in Japan, looking both at interactions in tuberculosis wards and housing estates. Figure 8.3 is drawn from one of his studies. The figure shows the amount of acquaintanceship between people whose beds were in different locations and indicates quite clearly the effect of relatively small architectural variables on this.

8.6. *Theory and Some Architectural Implications*

From the research described above it is clear that space use plays an active role in human interaction. As Altman[16] points out, the use of space may be considered both as determined *by* people and a determiner *of* human behaviour. But what can we say about its role? We have seen that a simple and direct extrapolation from animal behaviour is not tenable and so we must look to other propositions which take account of uniquely human qualities, whilst still drawing upon the central principles underlying animal use of space. One possibility is that we use space as yet another medium of communication, that we use it to indicate our feelings of, or attitudes towards, the type of activity in which we intend to engage. In an experiment carried out by Porter *et al.*[22] specifically to test this possibility with regard to interpersonal proximity it was not possible to show that anything was communicated at all. Thus the fact that we may be able to interpret intentions or feelings from the use of space in some situation (as Little,[9] for instance, has shown) does not necessarily mean that we actively use space as a means of expression.

A different view comes from looking at the work initiated by Festinger and his colleagues.[17] In those studies a person's location influenced the information he received, the people he met and hence the friendships he made. If we accept that information is not spread evenly over the environment then the location a person is in will influence his relationship to that information. The Festinger studies showed this to be the case at the scale of building layouts. Does this interpretation make sense at the level of the smaller scale of the position of people in rooms? Certainly the relationship between eye contact and distance indicates the greater the distance between people the greater the amount of information they try to obtain by looking. It is also possible to interpret the various studies by Sommer as indicating that people arrange themselves in various positions in order to minimise or optimise the amount of information they receive from others. The patterns found in the studies, the places people locate themselves in space, also fits in with this information hypothesis. It fits provided we regard it as information balance, control over interaction, that people are trying to achieve when locating themselves at the periphery in restaurants, say, or near to pillars in public waiting places.

Accepting then that one of the major roles of human spatial behaviour is to control the quantities and quality of interaction in which a person will take part, what are the general implications for design?

One important implication comes from dismissing the analogy with animals. When designers accept this analogy there is a tendency for them to cast the users of their buildings in a subordinate role, as of a dog to its master. There is a tendency for them to assume that they know the hidden, innate forces which determine what people do and that they can thus manipulate these forces without the users being aware or being able to respond any differently than the designer wishes. Casting the user in an active role, trying to find a situation which optimises the balance between the communications, or information, which he wants to receive and which he wants to give, forces the designer to think more carefully about the people who will be using his building. Why they will be there. What they will be doing and how they will be doing it. Unlike the New England warblers people are able to talk to one another and to agree amongst themselves how they will use the space available to them.

QUESTIONS FOR DISCUSSION

(1) In what ways can the design of buildings: (a) enhance and (b) reduce territorial-like behaviour in people?

(2) How would you expect discussions around a circular table to differ from those around a square table?

(3) Try to make some observations of the distance you see people sitting from each other on seats such as park benches. What can you infer from these observations: (a) about the relationships between the people, (b) about the utilisation of similar bench space in crowded and semi-crowded conditions?

(4) Do you think the nature of the role you have in your present organisation would change if the location of the place in which you spend the majority of your time were different?

(5) Are there any analogies with animals which would help to explain your answer to Question 4?

Chapter 9

Organisation

9.1. A Change of Direction

In the late 1920s as the depression was approaching, a series of investigations were carried out at the Hawthorne Works of the Western Electric Company.[1] These studies had the fairly mundane and very commercial aim of clarifying under what working conditions production would be highest. Such things as lighting and length of rest pauses were modified and the changes in the behaviour of the workers noted. Well-known physiologists and electrical engineers were involved in the project. They were there to ensure that the maximum productivity could be extracted from the workers by using the environment in the most effective way. Whatever subsequent interpretations and re-interpretations have been made of this study (*e.g.* Landsberger, Reference 2) we can look on it, justifiably, as the first major series of environmental psychology field experiments. The fact that these investigations considerably slowed down environmental psychology for perhaps thirty years just shows how devious and surprising the scientific study of people can be.

The reasons why the Hawthorne investigations caused such a dramatic change in the direction of studies of behaviour in industry are many and complex, but the most obvious was the fact that the investigators could show no simple relationship between working conditions and performance. In one experiment carried out in a room in which small parts were inspected, the investigators steadily increased the illumination, the production of the workers was found to increase but in a surprisingly erratic way. In another study the lighting was steadily decreased until it was clearly insufficient, and yet efficiency was maintained. Indeed in one experiment the lighting was reduced to the level of moonlight and no noticeable effect on production was found.

Fortunately for future generations of factory workers (and the Western *Electric* Company) it was not assumed that electric lighting was unnecessary and that future factories should instead be provided with candelabra. Rather a search was made for other explanations of the unexpected results. This search led to a reconsideration of the conditions under which the experiments were conducted.

In order to ensure that the performance of the workers was as carefully monitored as possible and to facilitate the precise control of the experimental manipulations, some degree of reorganisation of the various working situations had taken place. Some groups of workers were put in separate rooms. For others conditions were varied within one room but they were directly aware of the variations being introduced. An investigator was stationed in each room and discussed at frequent intervals with the workers the conditions to which they were being subjected and their feelings about them. It dawned on the Hawthorne investigators that the critical determinants of changes in performance were the contacts with the investigators and involvement in the process of being studied. This 'Hawthorne effect', that is the interfering effect upon behaviour produced simply by observing that behaviour, has passed into the folklore of popular psychology. Paradoxically it changed the direction of industrial psychology away from the study of physical surroundings, and towards the study of interpersonal relationships and communication networks. Yet it does have many important implications for the design of the physical environment.

These implications are sometimes forgotten in the excitement over the consequences for the study of human relations. The Hawthorne results did actually show relationships between environment and behaviour. The behavioural changes did not have a direct and simple environmental cause, simply forcing the workers to work more or less effectively whether they were interested in so doing or not. The behavioural changes related to the workers' *interpretation* of the environmental modifications. It was what these modifications indicated about the relationships between management and workers that mattered.

Other implications for environmental designers stem from the fact that these studies showed the effect of interpersonal relationships upon productivity. The importance of this relates to that which has always made architects more similar to stage directors or film producers than to sculptors or composers. It is an essential part of their profession to communicate and co-operate with a wide range of other people. Once the level of sophistication is reached in which a person needs somebody else's assistance in order to produce a building, then it is useful to think of the building as the product of an organisation rather than the creation of an individual. In the present complex technological society all buildings are the products of a number of inter-related organisations. Thus the lessons of organisational psychology, which have grown out of the industrial psychology of the Hawthorne studies, is directly pertinent to the business of being an architect.

There is another reason why architects should look at organisational psychology in more detail than they have been prone to in the past. All buildings house organisations. The *performance* of a building has even been defined as the degree to which it enables the organisation it houses to operate effectively.[3]

9.2. *What is an Organisation?*

Whenever two or more people need to work together in order to achieve some common goal then we have an organisation. But even in a two man organisation, say for example, a man building his house from local, natural materials with only the aid of his neighbour, many of the problems of large scale organisations can be seen. For instance, some proportion of the energies of the people of whom the organisation consists must be devoted simply to co-ordinating their activities. The two neighbours must agree upon the sequence in which they will build the building or obtain materials for it. In order to do this there must be some communication. Thus, it follows from the above definition of an organisation that one of the crucial factors in its operation is the form and nature of the communications which take place between its members.

A second level of complexity is reached when an organisation grows to the degree that one individual must spend a large part of his time monitoring and co-ordinating the actions of the others. This complexity arises partly out of the fact that the individual in the 'management' position must also monitor and control the communications between the other members of the organisation. This requires that communications must now carry some information about the communication processes themselves, further increasing the load upon them.

A third level of complexity is achieved when two organisations at the second level must interact with one another. In this situation, as we shall see in more detail later, the actual position within the communication network of the liaising individuals is quite crucial. These individuals must be able to understand the communication processes within their organisation in order to ensure that they can adequately represent it when contacting their partner organisation.

It is thus apparent that it is difficult to study organisations without considering communication. Any communication channel can be thought of as having a number of distinct properties, some of the most important being, first, the type of information it can carry and, secondly, the amount of information. When the communication is between two people it is also often the case that there is a preferred direction for communications. They can often flow from senior to junior levels of management, for instance, more readily than the other way around. It is also important to recognise that when we are considering communication between people rather than between, say, computers, a considerable amount of subtlety is possible in the variations between the channels available. Intensity of emotional reactions may be more easily transmitted through the observation of another person's bodily movements and facial expressions than by reading a written account, for instance. On the other hand, specific and detailed information is more easily carried on paper than in the head.

A further complication arises when considering people which is not so obvious when considering machines. The actual nature of the source from which the communication comes, and the recipient for whom it is intended, play a large part in determining the efficiency and effectiveness of the communication. People will modify their message in the light of their understanding of or attitudes towards the person they see as the main recipient of that message.

One thing which is very important in influencing the communications transmitted and received is *role*. In fact role may be defined simply as position within a communication network, higher status people usually having more central positions. However, as the day to day roles we come across are placed within the complex communication network of the whole society more detailed differentiation is possible and necessary. One way in which we differentiate roles is in terms of the usual types of information with which people in that role deal. For instance, we assume that architects deal mainly with visual information whereas quantity surveyors are thought of as dealing with numbers. Where these role perceptions are accurate they facilitate communication by ensuring that the right type and amount of information is transmitted to the right person. However, if they are wrong they can cause great confusion as they will inhibit the correct flow and encourage information to be transmitted to people who cannot deal with it. If, for instance, the quantity surveyor needs to see the configuration of the site for a building, yet this is never shown to him, because it is felt that he can only understand numbers, then big errors may be made. If, on the other hand, bills of quantity are usually sent direct to the architect then it is possible that he will misinterpret them and hence use them inefficiently. In order to obviate these sorts of difficulties it is necessary for the organisation to have a degree of *adaptability* within its structure, but this in turn will depend on the patterns of communication which take place within it.

This need for adaptability conflicts to some degree with the need for *identity*. If it is necessary to identify the role a person has in order to facilitate communication, then variations in that role over time due to adaptation will only cause confusion. A balance must therefore be found between these two in order to give the organisation some *stability*.

Adaptability, stability and identifiability may be regarded as the three key aspects of an organisation which enable it to survive. The various parts of which the organisation is composed must also possess them in the right proportions. One further thing is necessary in order for an organisation to exist and continue existing. This can be derived from our original definition of an organisation. People must need to work within it. In other words they must get some satisfaction from being functioning members of their organisation. This fourth key aspect of an organisation is therefore the levels of *satisfaction* of its workers, their morale.

9.3. Worker Satisfaction

The study of job satisfaction may be thought of as a study of *why* people work, or more colloquially as studies of 'what's in it for the workers'. Whilst this type of study grew out of the discovery by the Hawthorne investigators that wages were not the sole motivator, it received an impetus from the awareness in World War II that morale was a very important factor in the effectiveness of combat teams. This awareness was translated back into industry by trying to isolate the main determinants of worker satisfaction. Initially it was thought that high satisfaction would produce high productivity but as we shall see this is not necessarily the case.

The feasibility of carrying out large scale factor analyses, due to the availability of computers, enabled the underlying dimensions of worker satisfaction to be isolated by analysing questionnaires in much the same way as described in Chapter 6. A large number of workers answered lengthy questionnaires dealing with feelings about their job. From a variety of studies seven commonly occurring dimensions have been isolated.[4, 5]

9.3.1. THE JOB ITSELF.—The actual work in which a person engages provides an important component of his overall satisfaction. This will relate to how interesting or varied the job is and the degree to which the person feels it is the right sort of job for him; that it is demanding enough.

9.3.2. CO-WORKERS.—As was very clear from the Hawthorne investigations, the people with whom a person has frequent contact during his working day provide an important determinant of how much he likes his job. Whether he shares common interests with them, finds them friendly or understanding, can be quite critical in influencing how satisfied a person is with his lot. An interesting study by Van Zelst[6] showed that house builders who were organised into teams on the basis of their patterns of friendship produced significantly more buildings than those who were organised into teams at random.

9.3.3. SUPERVISION.—One of the most important individuals who determines a person's job satisfaction is his supervisor or the person to whom he is immediately responsible. The most effective size for a working group relates among other things to the number of people with whom a supervisor can most readily cope. The supervisor, or leader of the work team, not only controls the patterns of interaction between the team members but also the flow of information and material from the rest of the organisation. In a study by Morse[7] it was found that variations in both satisfaction and productivity were most readily linked to the style of supervision.

9.3.4. THE ORGANISATION.—Attitudes towards the organisation in general, its image and that of its products, are often more important for its members than is realised. Indeed in many cases it may be that advertising has more of an impact in enhancing employees' feelings about the people for whom they work than in attracting prospective buyers. As Argyris[8] has discussed in some detail, one of the most central conflicts within any organisation is that between the individual's aims and goals and those of the organisation. He also points out that this can be a productive conflict, leading both individual and organisation to adapt to changing circumstances and thus survive. Thus, workers' attitudes towards their organisation are in many cases an important index of organisational effectiveness.

9.3.5. FINANCIAL REWARD.—It is often believed that wages or salaries are the only important determinants of job satisfaction. Most industrial conflict seems to be about wages and this leads to the impression that this is all that concerns most people. In a competitive commercially oriented society, complaining about money is socially acceptable, even expected. So it would not be surprising if grievances with financial reward were used in situations in which a general feeling of dissatisfaction exists. The evidence for this suggestion is difficult to establish but it is now clear that financial reward is only one of the many determinants of job satisfaction.

9.3.6. WORKING CONDITIONS.—As we have seen, the Hawthorne investigations were aimed specifically at finding the effects on production of working conditions. This they were not able to establish clearly. What they could establish however was that modifications of the working conditions carried implications for the workers and influenced their attitudes towards their jobs. Later studies have shown that working conditions are an identifiable aspect of overall worker satisfaction. Under the heading of working conditions is included a wide range of things from the length of coffee breaks to the decor of the canteen, but as was illustrated in Chapter 6 the actual physical environment can also be identified as a separate aspect of job satisfaction.

9.3.7. SELF-FULFILMENT.—Depending upon the method of analysis employed, self-fulfilment may be shown to be either the central dimension of which all others are a part, or as a separate factor clearly distinguishable from the rest. Either way, the degree to which the worker feels that he is getting recognition for his abilities and has the possibility of developing and advancing according to his merit is an important consideration.

9.3.8. THE QUESTION OF RELATIVE IMPORTANCE.—The relative importance of the above aspects of job satisfaction varies from job to job and individual to individual. It is therefore not profitable to provide a ranking which should be used generally for all buildings or during the whole design process. However, Blai[9] has shown that if satisfaction is assumed to relate to needs which can be arranged in a hierarchy from the most basic to the most transcendental (e.g. from the need for safety or security, through the need for acceptance, to the need for self-fulfilment), then people at different levels in an organisation have dominant needs at different levels in this hierarchy.

Herzberg et al.[10] have suggested that satisfactions obtained from work are really of two sorts. They either provide satisfaction or they provide dissatisfaction. It is suggested that financial reward and working conditions can only really hope to cause dissatisfaction when they are low. They will never cause positive satisfaction when they are high. On the other hand, recognition by fellow workers or self fulfilment can give rise to increases in satisfaction as they increase. One criticism of this view worth noting is that it is possible that very high levels of the 'dissatisfiers' are necessary to cause positive satisfaction and that these levels are rarely reached. The lack of satisfaction caused by working conditions, for instance, may thus be more an indictment of present day architecture than a fundamental aspect of human behaviour.

9.3.9. SATISFACTION AND PRODUCTIVITY.—We are now in a better position to examine the relationship between satisfaction and productivity. March and Simon[11] discussing this relationship in some detail drew a distinction between actual production on the job and the decision to continue working. In other words a distinction between day to day productivity and turnover. They argue that productivity on the job is controlled by many organisational forces such as the rate of flow of materials, the skill or experience of the worker, and so on. As a consequence, given the effects of these controlling forces, there is little leeway for job satisfaction to have any impact.

On the other hand the decision to work or not, to take advantage of slack supervision in order to take unscheduled rests or to take advantage of slight illness to stay off work, have all been found to relate closely to job satisfaction. Indeed in many studies turnover rates or amount of absenteeism have been taken as indices of the level of satisfaction within the organisation. The reason for this close relationship is that satisfaction, as we have defined it, is the reason for being a member of the organisation. If it is not provided then the organisation has no power to cause the worker to remain a member.

9.4. Networks of Communication

Not surprisingly a large proportion of the above aspects of job satisfaction are concerned with the individuals with whom contacts occur or from whom information is received. As a consequence the patterns of communication that these interactions follow would be expected to have a large impact on the effectiveness of the organisation and the satisfaction of the individuals who are part of it. Psychologists have studied these patterns of interaction and their effects in the laboratory by creating teams of different structures, under controlled conditions.

The main form of control is to limit both the *type* of communication which can be transmitted between team members and to *whom* the message can be sent. By this means a great variety of patterns can be produced. Figure 9.1 illustrates three of the basic patterns which have been examined. In Figure 9.1(a) all members of the team can contact all other members so that a fairly open democratic team is possible. The team illustrated in Figure 9.1(b) would only become democratic if the person at position E tried to make it so.

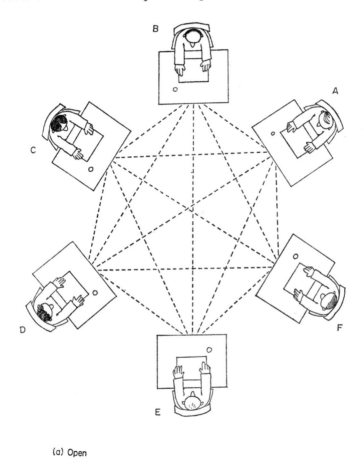

(a) Open

Fig. 9.1(a)

All information must pass through him and so a hierarchical structure is produced. The straight line structure shown in Figure 9.1(c) is an interesting one because although the people at positions C or D can take on roles similar to that of the person at position E,

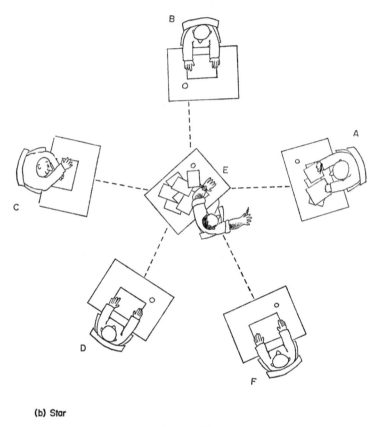

(b) Star

Fig. 9.1(b)

in Figure 9.1(b), they are still much more dependent on their people at B and E. So it is possible with such a structure that a level similar perhaps to junior management can develop at positions B and D effectively making A and F the 'shop floor'. A number of other possible developments can occur with the line arrangement and if

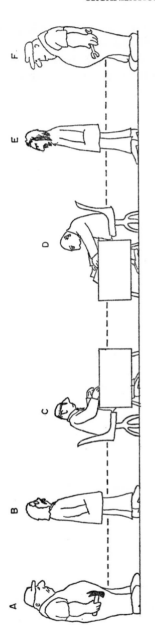

Fig. 9.1(c)

(c) Line

the two ends are joined as is illustrated in Figure 9.1(d) then almost any individual can find himself in a dominant role.

Table 9.1 shows the results of one study in which the teams were each designing a children's playground using standard equipment. By looking at the ratio of messages sent to those received, the

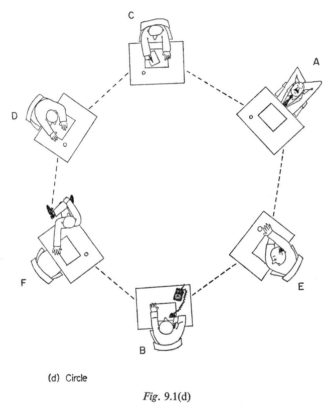

(d) Circle

Fig. 9.1(d)

Fig. 9.1. Patterns of communication.

differences in the part played by each member as a result of his position in the network may be seen. The person represented by each letter in this table was given the same information and role designation so changes in the flow of messages related simply to the people he was allowed to contact.

The communications between individuals in these experiments are often limited to written messages. This is both in order to slow the process down to facilitate observation and recording and to magnify the effects of the communication network. The tasks the team are given can be thought of as either open ended, in which there is no correct answer but in which an answer of some novelty

Table 9.1

Effects of communication structure on flow of messages as shown by percentage of messages sent to those received

Person	Structure		
	Open	Star	Circle
A	68	175	110
B	110	303	130
C	105	61	90
D	161	230	96
E	71	83	75
F	161	330	109

(*See* Figures 9.1(a), (b) and (d))

or originality is sought, or specific, in which there is one correct answer (*e.g.* a mathematical problem or an anagram). Each member of the team is given different information relevant to the task. It is up to the team to communicate with each other according to the rules of contact laid down and to present a solution.

When described coldly like this these experiments seem very artificial, but, as the many people who have taken part in them will agree, they very quickly come to life and take on a reality of their own. Many unscheduled things happen which are accurate reflections of the real world: people go on strike, informal unofficial groups form and the messengers, ostensibly working for the experimenters, become involved in team struggles. As our former consideration of communications suggested, this situation may be enhanced by defining the roles of the team members more precisely and by giving them a task that relates to a specific profession. In exercises which I have developed for architects, people have been told they are for example a 'civil engineer', 'landscape architect' or 'planning officer of the local authority'. The team has been asked to make a decision about the design of, say, a children's playground or a Japanese rock garden. Each member is given different pieces of information such as the cost of equipment or the site plan, such that a workable solution is only possible by combining all the material. Furthermore, by modifying this information and the original instructions, it is possible to make the solution more specific or more open-ended. An 'adventure playground' with high cost limits, for instance, would provide a more open-ended problem than a conventional playground on a small site, for in the latter case only one solution may be possible. When the reality of the situation is increased by doing this people can become involved and the exercise becomes a very real experience for those taking part.

It is not surprising to find that these exercises relate closely to the real world because there are many decisions which are taken outside of the laboratory that follow similar patterns. Just to take the architectural decision-making process as an example, it is rare indeed for all the people involved in the decision, the designers, contractors, clients, local authority inspectors, etc., all to meet together in open discussion about the building concerned. Many people would be horrified at the thought of such a committee meeting and so quite consciously develop communication structures that will obviate them. Furthermore, a great deal of information must be transmitted on paper with all the resultant complications. In some cases all the people involved in the design of the building will know each other and feel free to contact one another. For instance, if the services engineer is a little worried about the cost of a modification he may contact the quantity surveyor directly. In other cases all communication must pass through the architect's office and he might ensure that it goes to the right person. However, it is only when the structures which exist are isolated in the laboratory that their nature and influence can be appreciated.

A variety of measurements can be made of the activities and attitudes of a team and its members. These can include the length of time it takes them to produce a solution, the amount and type of information which passes between different members and the satisfaction of the individual members with their own part in the team's activities. One of the most interesting findings which consistently came out of these studies is the relationship between all these different measures.[12,13]

In order to see some of the complexities of the processes involved in these small group problem-solving teams, it is probably easiest to look first at the star configuration as in Figure 9.1(b). A typical occurrence in this configuration is that considerable pressure is put upon E, the man at the centre. He receives far more messages than he can cope with and consequently he feels overworked whilst the other members of the team feel under-utilised. It is also quite common for E to develop a working understanding with one or two members of the team with a consequent further detriment in the role played by the remainder. In fact the only way for E to escape from his dilemma is either to ignore a number of members of his team or to act simply as a communications centre, passing on messages but being relatively little involved in decision making.

If we look at the line or circle configuration (Figures 9.1(c) or (d)) we can see that there is frequently a similar tendency to that found in the star. One individual becomes dominant and proceeds to take command with the assistance of those adjacent to him, the rest being left out of the decisions. The alternative to this, of keeping everyone in the team in contant contact with everyone else, leads to a great deal of confusion. This confusion is typical of configuration (a) in which everybody has contact with everybody else. In the latter case no one individual can see that he is in a dominant role by virtue of his position in the network, and so considerable effort may be devoted to trying to give the team a structure by which decisions can be made.

If an individual's satisfaction with his role on the team and his team's performance is examined, it is usually found to relate closely to the structure of the team in which he was and his position in that team. People who find themselves in central positions feel that they had an important role in the exercise and are satisfied with their contribution to it, whereas those on the periphery are considerably less so. As a consequence, members of the configuration in which everyone can contact everyone else are generally more satisfied with themselves and their team than are the members of the circle configuration. The members of the star who are not at the centre are usually the most dissatisfied of all. In fact with the exercises I have run it is not at all uncommon for these peripheral members to get very angry and rude, sending increasingly irate messages to their centre man. This introduces more confusion and puts more pressure on him so that he often dismisses their contribution entirely and as a consequence leads to their dismissal of the whole exercise. One typical example of the *last* message sent from D to E is 'I have now handed in my notice, and resigned. Up yours!'

This state of disarray is of course an extreme example of an organisation breaking down because of an ineffective communications system, but it illustrates clearly how important it is for group leaders (or supervisors) to keep their subordinates involved and satisfied if they are to keep them as productive and effective members of their team. (The effects of environment on interaction considered in Chapter 8 have some bearings on this.) Even in the artificial exercise that we have been looking at, a number of unscheduled activities occur that enable us to understand the processes which develop in organisation to give people some level of satisfaction. The messengers who distribute the communications often become involved in the process and are encouraged to contact people with whom the transmitter is not really allowed to be in contact. In the star configuration, D will try to get in touch with C just to feel that he is not forgotten. In the circle, B will contact D because he feels it is the only way out of the muddle. This is directly analogous to the whole range of informal contacts which are found in all formal organisations. Besides keeping the morale of the workers from sinking too low, they also provide the organisation with a flexibility, or adaptability, that it might not otherwise have.

Of course the most successful decision-making structure depends upon the type of decision in which the group is involved. A task which really has one preferred, recognisable solution will probably be dealt with more readily by the sort of autocratic team represented by the star. On the other hand, a task with a more open-ended solution that requires some sort of originality will probably be dealt with more effectively by a group in which all the members are actively involved. The interesting thing is that if the individual members of the group are very goal oriented, that is, keen to come up with a solution, then they will accept or even call for an autocratic structure if they feel this structure will help them produce that solution. We can thus see that the supervisor's role, the role of other people and the job itself, which we found earlier to be important aspects of job satisfaction, can all be seen to have roots in the communication structures of small working groups. As a consequence the success of many groups can be traced to the degree to which the patterns of communication are appropriate for the tasks. A group which is aware of its structure and attempts to modify it to make it more appropriate is often more successful than one which does not.

The early messages which flow within a group also help to give us some indication of the way people come to terms with being group members. The first message transmitted is usually 'who are you?' This is an attempt to find the location of the person in the communication structure and the role associated with it. This in its turn will help the person to decide what type of interaction to enter into with the people with whom he is communicating. It is no accident that the question 'who are you?', or parallel questions, are also the first to be asked when meeting strangers at a party. For it is only when we have got the beginnings of the answer to such a question that we have some idea how to deal with them. If the answer given accurately summarises the person to the degree that it helps us to predict how he will react to others at the party, or in the team exercise if it gives us some indications of his function in the team, then it can facilitate communication to a marked degree. However, in many cases it may only add confusion (add 'noise' to the system).

To explore this further in design exercises, two different approaches are often tried. In one condition the students taking part are given a title. A is told 'you are the architect' and B 'you are the landscape architect' and so on. In a second condition they are just given the information for the game but no designation. We have found that the differences show that there really is something in a name.

The person who is told he is the architect often takes over the leadership of the team and his instructions are followed even if he is in a poor position for instructing, such as the periphery of the star. On the other hand, in the open group when no roles are assigned, a great deal of effort often goes into trying to decide who is what. This is frequently determined on the basis of the information a person has rather than his position in the network.

One further important point about group functioning arises from examining the way in which groups interact with other groups. Of particular interest is the effect of location in his team's network on any individual who has to act as a link with other groups. This 'liaison' officer often really needs to be at a central place in the network if he is to do the job properly. He has to know how his organisation will cope with requests from others, how adaptable it is, what its communication structure is. In the real world it is frequently a very junior person who has this role, with resultant frustrations.

9.5. Types of Organisation

The two extreme types of structure we looked at above, the 'open' and the 'star', have their counterparts in actual organisations. Investigators such as Pugh et al. (1968, 1969) have even shown them to be related to aspects of two ends of an important organisational dimension. A dimension which runs from a full bureaucracy to one whose organisation is 'implicitly structured'. Every organisation has a more or less stable pattern of activity within it and a role structure with its concomitant specialisation in the tasks performed. If it did not it would not be possible to recognise it as a given organisation. The variations relate to the amount of centralisation in the communication and decision-making processes and the degree of rigidity of the definitions of the roles which make up the organisation.

The interesting point which Pugh and his colleagues have shown is that the different types of organisational structures (of course, he uses a much more detailed taxonomy than the one we have had time to look at here) relate to the size of the organisation and the type of things that it produces. Small organisations which produce things requiring a relatively simple technology tend to be less bureaucratic than the large organisations which use a complex technology. It also follows that their problems are different. Where the large organisations can often satisfy such aspects as working conditions and financial reward, it is in the areas of attitudes towards the organisation and self fulfilment that they are most likely to have difficulty with the majority of their employees. This is as would be expected from our discussion of communication networks.

9.6. Leadership and Architecture

The psychological literature on leadership is considerable (*see* for instance Gibbs[14]), but we must limit ourselves here to a brief consideration of the leader's (or manager's) role in an organisation, from the viewpoint of the topics we have been discussing and in particular from the definitions which this viewpoint gives to that role.

Examination of organisations reveals at least three distinct types of leader. The first, and possibly the one most usually referred to as the leader, is the person who is at the most central position in the communication (or decision making) network. Because of his position this person is usually the one from whom actions (or decisions) are seen to emanate. Other individuals who might want to initiate actions frequently have to do so through this central person, further enhancing his leadership role.

The second aspect of leadership relates to the information available and the means of using it. As we have seen, it is possible for someone on the periphery of the communication network to possess most of the crucial information (especially if his role is assigned independently of his position in the network). Because he possesses this information, he may initiate action (or 'lead' the team or organisation). Indeed, it is quite common for groups to function with one person who has the information, but is peripheral, and another who does not have much information, but is central, working closely with one another. The division of these two aspects of leadership often seems to strengthen the leadership of the group as a whole.

However, we have also seen that a clearer decision-making hierarchy has a tendency to lower the satisfaction of the lower members of that hierarchy. A third and important aspect of leadership may then be loosely thought of as 'keeping people happy'. For it is only in keeping their satisfaction at an acceptable level that they will continue as members of the organisation. The very existence of the organisation can thus depend on this type of leadership.

It is rare for one individual to take on all of these aspects of leadership and succeed. It is likely that in all groups which function well, all individuals take on all of the roles at different times. A problem which has yet to be resolved by the architectural profession is the nature of its leadership of the building process. We saw in the first chapter that the architect's role is a complex one. He ranges from being the centre of the communication network to being the person who keeps the client happy. The message of this chapter is that different forms of leadership and communication structure are better for different tasks. Quite different tasks are dealt with at different stages in the design process. Too rigid role definition can lead to malfunction.

9.7. Summary and Conclusions

This chapter has shown us that the psychological processes underlying organisations have two distinct components. These are the structure of the communications within the organisation and the satisfaction of the members which motivates them to continue to be members.

One of the clear implications from this work for architects, as we have just seen, is that leadership relates to a wide range of factors affecting group functioning. Thus the leadership of the building team and the role of the architect himself could bear some reconsideration in relation to the concepts touched on in this chapter.

As regards the actual buildings produced, it can be seen that in accommodating organisations a wide range of types and patterns of communication must be considered together with a variety of satisfactions. That architectural entities take on meanings, as we have seen in a number of previous chapters, when taken together with the ideas presented in this chapter, help to reveal some of the rather subtle ways in which buildings enable organisations to survive.

QUESTIONS FOR DISCUSSION

By far the best way to explore further the issues raised in this chapter is to try to carry out the exercises illustrated. Gather together five or six interested people and give each some information relating to a common problem (anagrams, crosswords or simple design problems are all readily used material). Then structure the communications between them according to the networks described. By this or other means the following are some of the questions which would be worth exploring:

(1) How does behaviour differ if people are aware of the network as opposed to groups who do not know what the network is?

(2) How does behaviour differ if people are given named roles, which either agree or disagree with the information they have, to those in groups in which no positions are named?

(3) How does the time available influence how the group organises itself?

(4) What conditions enhance an overload of communications on one individual?

Some further issues which arise from this chapter are:

(5) In what real world decision-making situations is the network known, unknown, and a role specification known or unknown?

(6) What are the implications for this knowledge or lack of it for building design?

(7) How do (might) senior design partners ensure (increase) the satisfactions of their subordinates?

(8) What aspects of the designer's office layout might influence the answers to Question 4?

Chapter 10

Some Design Problems Considered

10.1. Concluding Introduction

Unlike most attempts to introduce psychology to architects, in this book I have taken psychology as my starting point and source of reference, rather than architecture. I have not plucked problems from design decision making and attempted to find answers in psychology. Instead, I have attempted to provide a psychological framework within which it should be possible not only to begin answering architectural problems but, more importantly, to facilitate their formulation. A man living on a small roadless island could learn to drive a car. However, the skill would be almost useless to him in a modern city because he would have no idea of how to cope with the problems of road traffic and city navigation. Similarly many architects enter some area of environmental or architectural psychology, achieve a certain competence but can never use their skills effectively because they do not understand the terrain of which their chosen area is a part. It is also, of course, a great temptation to an increasing number of psychologists to jump into the heady waters of architecture (if a change of metaphor is permitted), without mapping fully the eddies and undercurrents. To psychologists, architecture provides the scale and possibilities of real world decision making so sadly lacking in their laboratories. It would thus have been most inviting to me to have specified the way I would like to see buildings produced, and to cloak my opinions in psychological jargon. However, I don't think that to be the most useful contribution of a psychologist. None the less, many readers will still be asking how psychology can or does help to solve those problems formulated by architects in ignorance of the matters discussed in this book. By way of responding to this I will take two specific issues within architectural design and use them to illustrate in a little more detail the ways in which concepts and information from previous chapters might be used.

Before doing this it must be emphasised once again that this brief book touches upon only a few areas of psychology and even in those areas it has rarely been possible to give detailed consideration. Furthermore, it should be clear by now that much of academic psychology has developed if not in ignorance of the physical environment then at least without paying much attention to it. Thus there is a tremendous amount of work to be done both in the development of psychological concepts and in carrying out the necessary research before a discipline will emerge which will be seen to contribute directly to the processes of design.

10.2. Windows

The first architectural issue I will look at is that of windows. Most buildings have windows. Those without are considered unusual and, by some, possibly evil. Their size and shape influence to a marked degree the appearance of the facade of a building, and because the qualities of the internal environment usually derive from them, they influence both the shape of buildings and the way in which those buildings are arranged in relation to one another. Thus an understanding or even a questioning of the psychological implications of windows could have a marked impact upon many aspects of the design of buildings. Small changes in our orientation towards them could alter the shape of cities as we know them.

Our method of dealing with windows will be to break their psychological implications into meaningful components so that we can answer the question: 'What are windows for?', 'What functions (particularly psychological ones) do they serve?' We will then see what the answers to this question implies.

In the light of earlier discussions it is clear that there are a number of processes which need to be differentiated from each other if we are to answer this question at all coherently. We must clarify whether we are dealing with aspects of human performance, whether we are dealing with perceptual judgements or whether it is really the meaning associated with windows (the dimensions underlying our attitudes towards them) and the relationship which that meaning has to various aspects of satisfaction which is our concern. Furthermore, it is clear that during the course of development people will learn behaviour patterns in relation to windows and will consequently also have learnt associations with them.

From the viewpoint of human performance it would seem that windows provide the opportunity for light of certain types at certain angles and with a certain degree of variability and also often the opportunity of a reasonable control over ventilation. Whilst little attention has been paid in this book to the relationships between the physical environment and actual performance it should be apparent that within relatively broad levels little direct relationship can be found. The Hawthorne[1] investigations showed that people could perform remarkably well under very low light levels and much research since those times has indicated that unless we are dealing with very specific tasks (such as visual acuity tests) then variations in light level have little direct effect. Even if they did, modern artificial lighting systems are built to provide reasonable levels quite effectively. Performance does relate to small variations in temperature[2] and in this respect it would seem that the degree of control afforded by the possibility of opening windows is worth bearing in mind in our general discussion. But besides this aspect of control over ventilation what other properties are there which might be expected to influence performance? Variations in light level could conceivably help to keep people awake but there again artificial variations could be introduced.

A different argument for the function of windows, which is often put forward by architects, is that windows satisfy the need to keep contact with the outside. Little has been said in this book about basic human needs, but it has been argued that there are probably very few aspects of human behaviour which can be related directly to innate mechanisms, or which have their origins in our animal ancestry. The only *basic* needs which can be clearly identified are those rather obvious ones which contribute directly to survival, the physiological needs for food, sleep and, possibly, sex.

What can contact with the outside offer? It can provide us with information about changes in the diurnal and seasonal patterns and information about such things as the weather. It can also provide in some cases an interesting and varied view. In what ways can these properties be expected to contribute directly to performance? We have seen in the previous chapter that there is little evidence for a simple relationship between satisfaction and performance and so if the information or view provided were to contribute only to satisfaction we would not expect them to influence performance directly.

We can thus see that we would not expect the presence or absence of windows to influence performance, and although there has been little research, what research there has been[3] supports this proposition. Yet people and in particular architects seem to hold strong views about the presence or absence of windows. What are the roots of these views? To approach an answer to this it is necessary to consider some of the other psychological processes referred to above. As regards perceptual judgements how might windows help? And in relation to what judgements?

Judgements of what goes on inside a building and more aesthetically related judgements as to pleasantness of form are inevitably influenced by the patterning of materials, glass amongst them, which make up the facade of the building. But besides the ability to see into the building, which the occupants frequently reduce, there would seem to be nothing intrinsically related to windows which contributes to these perceptual judgements. Furthermore, as we saw in the chapter on perception, the shapes and forms which exist are not likely to have an innate effect. However it does seem possible that glass might be one frequently occurring material which is helpful in providing perceptual structure and form to a configuration of building materials, interestingly enough, however, it is often the solidity of windows caused by reflections which most enhance this. Mirrors would do the job better.

From the inside of a building judgements about where you are do seem likely to relate to the type of rich information which is at present often provided by a view out. Buildings in which long internal corridors exist without windows are often found to be very disorienting for newcomers. But here again we can see that there is nothing unique about this attribute provided by windows, it could be provided in a number of other ways (*e.g.* colour coding, good signposting?). It is just the case that generally speaking a rich variety of stimuli which vary with the time of day and year has been provided in the past by means of windows.

Perhaps then it is in the area of previous learning or expectancies that we can find the characteristic value of windows? Certainly in the past large windows overlooking country scenes had a direct association with a certain quality of life, status and so on. Furthermore, the technical possibilities and the costs associated with them were much more restricted in the past. It is likely that our views about, or attitudes towards, windows have grown up in relation to the implications of these limitations (*e.g.* wealth or modernity). However, this aspect, like all the others we have considered, is not an inevitable part of windows nor can it be supplied only by windows.

Thus by examining, admittedly in general terms, the psychological functions which windows may fulfil we have seen that there is no single property which is unique to windows. We could make our examination more specific by reference to particular aspects and earlier chapters. For instance, for 'what individuals are our arguments most convincing?' 'What learnt habits, in relation to what patterns of reinforcement, are associated with them?' But from the above argument we may consequently reach the not so obvious conclusion that windows are not, psychologically speaking, necessary for buildings! Further, if they were to be used for specific functions, such as view or ventilation, then quite different windows and hence buildings and cities would be produced. Of course the functions which windows do serve would still need to be satisfied in windowless buildings. The fact that this is rarely done, for instance by providing varied and large scale internal views, is possibly one reason why there seems to be such antagonism towards windowless environments. Anyone still in doubt as to the function of windows should consider large department stores or Japanese houses, two very different building types both traditionally 'windowless'. It thus seems likely that we have windows today because although no single aspect is essential, the practical possibilities of the situation dictate that *when taken together* windows are the easiest ways of achieving them. Furthermore it is highly probable that, over the years, out of this *combination* of properties, existing attitudes have grown.

From our general, simple argument a vision of vast, fascinating, internal cities unlike any today could be developed. However, as an empirical psychologist I am well aware of the gap between vision and reality and how it is filled with people making decisions. None the less, decisions do relate to information, analysis and argument. In architecture psychology is the starting point for all three.

10.3. Living Off the Ground

Of the many aspects of design about which psychological queries have been raised, the use of multi-storey dwellings is one over which some of the most vehement arguments have been waged. Indeed many planning authorities in Britain seem in the past few years to have decided not to build any more multi-storey housing. This about-turn from the post-war years would appear to be based on psychological assumptions.

What sort of assumptions are these and what are their validity?

One of the commonly occurring ones which is presented by architects is the 'need' which people have to be 'on the ground'. On a number of occasions I have questioned both the existence and the real meaning of these assumed needs. It is clear in this case for instance that throughout the history of civilised man he has spent a very small proportion of his time on real earth. What then is the difference between being 1 metre off the 'ground' and 10 or 100 metres off it? Is this a difference which relates to some basic need?

As we learn from our experience of buildings through childhood, height off the ground usually relates to our dependence upon machines, such as lifts, which are often far from perfectly reliable and to our removal in time and effort from many of the amenities of the cities or towns in which we live. Thus from a purely functional viewpoint the effects of living off the ground are not an inevitable part of the design but simply an aspect of the way in which high-rise buildings are produced today. The original conceptions behind them were quite different from the up-ended *cul-de-sacs* which are now produced.

Many of the other problems associated with high-rise development, such as the difficulties of finding the right sorts of places for informal contact outside of the home or for the ready access to the space provided by a garden, are not inevitable products of any high-rise development. It is just that the existing forms these take have those weaknesses.

Our examination of developmental psychology illustrated amongst other things the value for children of having the possibility of a variety of interactions with their physical surroundings. The way in which these interactions related to the location or presence of the mother also had an impact on behaviour. Clearly multi-storey dwellings as they exist today limit the range of interactions that are possible.

In this brief examination I have come closer to a straightforward functional view of our use of buildings and have possibly appeared to be arguing against a 'psychological' (even if a lay one) explanation of the failure of multi-storey buildings. But the contrast with my examination of windows should elucidate this. With windows I argued we could do without them, for high-rise buildings I argued they could be successful if differently designed. In both cases I have been at pains to *free* the architect from misplaced psychological assumptions. As I discussed in the first chapter, there are many such assumptions which inhibit design. But it should also now be clear, that to reach the rather down to earth levels at which we will find many of the truly psychological functions of buildings (certainly not all of them), we must first come to grips with some of the more abstract problems which form psychology.

10.4. The Model of Man

One way of summarising the contribution of psychology to architecture is by suggesting that, somewhat paradoxically, it is the view of man which psychology provides which is its greatest contribution. This is the view, in lay terms, of what 'makes people tick'. Or slightly more technically, the appropriate 'model of man'.

If a designer sees people as essentially passive, responding to the pressures of his building in a simple and direct way, then this will shape the building form which he produces. On the other hand a model which has its roots more directly in organic or biological analogies, which sees people as consciously trying to adapt to, and make sense of, their environment leads to a different (and often more indeterminate) type of architecture. The great dangers of the 'self-fulfilling' prophecy require that these models are brought out into the open and tested objectively. For instance, a building which limits the possibilities of adaptation will tend to encourage regular, unvaried behaviour. If the designer looks at this behaviour he will say; 'There I told you. People don't need adaptable buildings'. Thus a mechanical model of man on the part of the designer may lead to mechanical-like behaviour on the part of the users.

Here perhaps lies the strength of the academic psychologist's approach over the architectural practitioner. Where the architect can only really test the degree to which the patterns of behaviour, in the buildings he designs, fit his implicit or explicit views of how and why people behave, the academic, working with his abstract stimuli and often more or less independently of real world problems, can test and compare the basic models he has of how and why people behave as they do. His conclusions on this are the essence of what he has to pass on to those who must apply his findings.

10.5. By Way of Concluding

However fleetingly, we have in this book looked at human experience from many different viewpoints. In all cases an attempt has been made to link these views to the physical environment in which we find ourselves, in particular to the man-made environment. In the present chapter it has been shown by reference to two examples, that consideration of the findings and concepts from scientific psychology could have very profound influences both for the form of our buildings and for the way of life which they delineate. We have also seen that questioning the function of particular aspects of architecture almost inevitably leads to questions about the view of man which we hold.

This is as it should be. Buildings are for people. People build them, use them, administer them and pass them by. If our examination of psychology has shown us anything, it has shown us that it is possible to consider a people-oriented environment and has indicated that it might be feasible to produce one. The increasing awareness of the need for this has been one of the causes of the increase in research in this area but as usual it has been the daily news reports which have spotlighted the depths of our ignorance.

For instance, the fuss which Bobby Fisher made in his chess match with Boris Spassky has been seen as just another development in unorthodox opening gambits, but many people have missed the large role which environment played. At the largest scale the country for the match was disputed and at the smallest Fisher had his own chair flown in from America. Never has positional play shown so clearly the role of our physical surroundings in providing meaning for our actions.

Seemingly more frivolous but of greater moment, was the haggling at the Paris peace talks between the Vietnamese and American negotiators over the shape of the conference table. We can now see that the implications of table shape, and haggling over small scale environmental issues generally, may well be broader than often appreciated.

Possibly the most tragic case reported is that of the person who murdered his neighbour because of the continuous noise and insults he received from him. How might this tragic case have ended if the designers of the houses involved had had more consideration for the interactions between building users, for the interactions between buildings and users, and the varieties of those interactions which exist?

Review of Research

The following references are for those wishing to study architectural/environmental psychology further. They are limited to books which are readily available in English.

Reviews of the Literature

BELL, G., RANDALL, E. and ROEDER, J. E. R., *Urban Environments and Human Behaviour: An annotated bibliography,* Dowden, Hutchinson and Ross, Stroudsbury, 1973.

CANTER, D. V., 'Empirical research in environmental psychology: a brief review', *Bulletin of the British Psychological Society,* January (1974) (in press).

CRAIK, K. H., 'Environmental psychology', in (ed. K. H. Craik *et al.*), *New Directions in Psychology,* Holt, Rinehart and Winston, New York, 1970.

CRAIK, K. H., 'Environmental psychology', *Annual Review of Psychology,* **24,** 403–22 (1973).

WOHLWILL, J. F., 'The emerging discipline of environmental psychology', *American Psychologist,* **25,** 303–12 (1970).

Books of Readings

CANTER, D. V. (ed.) *Architectural Psychology,* RIBA, London, 1970.

CANTER, D. V. and LEE, T. R. (eds.) *Psychology and the Built Environment,* Architectural Press, London, 1974.

DOWN, R. M. and STEA, D. (eds.) *Image and Environment: Cognitive Mapping and Spatial Behaviour,* Aldine, Chicago, 1973.

ENGLISH, P. W. and MAYFIELD, R. C. (eds.) *Man, Space and Environment,* Oxford University Press, London, 1972.

ESSER, A. H. (ed.) *Behaviour and Environment: Use of Space by Animals and Men,* Plenum, New York, 1971.

EWALD, W. R. (ed.) *Environment for Man,* Indiana University, London, 1967.

GUTMAN, R (ed.) *People and Buildings,* Basic Books, New York, 1972.

ITTELSON, W. H. (ed.) *Environment and Cognition,* Seminar Press, New York, 1973.

LOWENTHAL, D. (ed.) *Environmental Perception and Behaviour,* University of Chicago Press, Chicago, 1967.

PASTALAN, L. and CARSON, D. H. (eds.) *Spatial Behaviour of Older People,* University of Michigan, Ann Arbor, 1970.

PROSHANSKY, H. M., ITTELSON, W. H. and RIVLIN, L. G. (eds.) *Environmental Psychology: Man and his Physical Setting,* Holt, Rinehart and Winston, New York, 1970.

WARD, C. (ed.) *Vandalism,* Architectural Press, London, 1973.

Conference Proceedings

ARCHEA, J. and EASTMAN, C. (eds.) *EDRA* Two,* Carnegie, Mellon University, Pittsburgh, 1970.

HONIKMAN, B. (ed.) *Proceedings of Architectural Psychology Conference at Kingston Polytechnic,* RIBA, London, 1971.

MITCHELL, W. J. (ed.) *Environmental Design: Research and Practice. EDRA Three,* University of California, Los Angeles, 1972.

PREISER, W. F. E. (ed.) *Environmental Design Research: Vol. one selected papers. EDRA Four,* Dowden, Hutchinson and Ross, Stroudsbury, 1973.

SANOFF, H. and COHN, S. (eds.) *EDRA One,* North Carolina State University, Raleigh, 1970.

Books on Specific Topics

BROADBENT, G., *Design in Architecture: Architecture and the Human Sciences,* Wiley, London, 1973.

BUILDING PERFORMANCE RESEARCH UNIT, *Building Performance,* Applied Science Publishers, London, 1972.

BURNS, W., *Noise and Man,* John Murray, London, 1968.

CAREY, L. and MAPES, R., *The Sociology of Planning: A Study of Social Activity on New Housing Estates,* Batsford, London, 1971.

LINDHEIM, R., GLASER, H. H. and COFFIN, C., *Changing Hospital Environments for Children,* Howard University, Cambridge, 1972.

LYNCH, K., *The Image of the City,* MIT Press, Cambridge, Mass., 1960.

MOLLER, C. B., *Architectural Environmental and our Mental Health,* Horizon, New York, 1968.

NEWMAN, O., *Defensible Space: People and Design in the Violent City,* Architectural Press, London, 1972.

PERIN, C., *With Man in Mind: An Interdisciplinary Prospectus for Environmental Design,* MIT Press, Cambridge, Mass., 1970.

RAPOPORT, A., *House Form and Culture,* Prentice-Hall, Englewood Cliffs, N.J., 1969.

RODDA, M., *Noise and Society,* Oliver and Boyd, London, 1967.

SOMMER, R., *Personal Space: The Behavioural Basis of Design,* Prentice-Hall, Englewood Cliffs, N.J., 1969.

Journals Oriented to Architectural/Environmental Psychology

Environment and Behaviour, Sage Publications, Beverley Hills, California.

Man–Environment Systems, Pennsylvania State University, University Park, Pennsylvania.

Journal of Architectural Research and Teaching, RIBA, London.

* EDRA is the Environmental Design Research Association.

References

Chapter 1

Further Reading

CANTER, D. V., 'Need for a theory of function in architecture', *Architects' Journal*, 4th February, 299–302 (1970).

LANGDON, J. F., 'The social and physical environment: a social scientist's view', *RIBA Journal*, **73**, 460–4 (1966).

LEE, T. R., 'Psychology and architectural determinism', *Architects' Journal*, 4th August, 253–62 (1971).

PROSHANSKY, H. M., ITTELSON, W. H. and RIVLIN, L. G., *Environmental Psychology: Man and his Physical Setting*, Holt, Rinehart and Winston, New York, 1970.

SOMMER, R., 'Can behavioural studies be useful as well as ornamental?', *Transactions of the Bartlett Society*, **5**, 49–65 (1966–7).

WELLS, B. W. P., 'Towards a definition of environmental studies: a psychologist's contribution', *Architects' Journal*, 22nd September, 677–9 (1965).

Chapter 2

References

1. CANTER, D. V., *The Psychological Implications of Office Design*, University of Liverpool: Ph.D. thesis. Other details may be found in; Canter, D. V., 'Office size: an example of psychological research in architecture', *Architects' Journal*, April, 881–8 (1968).

2. MANNING, P., *Office Design: A Study of Environment*, Pilkington Research Unit, Liverpool, 1965.

3. WELLS, B. W. P., 'Subjective responses to the lighting installation in a modern office building and their design implications', *Building Science*, **1**, 57–68 (1965).

4. BROADBENT, D. E., *Perception and Communication*, Pergamon, Oxford, 1946.

5. CAMPBELL, D. T. and FISKE, D. W., 'Convergent and discriminant validation by the multitrait-multimethod matrix', *Psychological Bulletin*, **56**, 81–105 (1959).

6. WITKIN, H. *et al.*, *Psychological Differentiation*, Wiley, London, 1962.

7. HAMMOND, K. R., 'Measuring attitudes by error choice: an indirect method,' *Journal of Abnormal Social Psychology*, **43**, 38–48 (1948).

8. WOOLS, R. and CANTER, D. V., 'The effects of the meaning of buildings on behaviour', *Applied Ergonomics*, **1**(3), 144–50 (1970).

Further Reading

CAMPBELL, D. J. and STANLEY, J. C., *Experimental and Quasi-Experimental Designs for Research*, Rand McNally, Chicago, 1963.

CANTER, D. V., 'On appraising building appraisals', *Architects' Journal*, 21st December, 881–8 (1966).

OPPENHEIM, A. N., *Questionnaire Design and Attitude Measurement*, Heinemann, London, 1966 (an elementary introduction).

SELLITZ, C., JAHODA, M., DEUTSCH, M. and COOK, S. W., *Research Methods in Social Relations*, Holt Rinehart, London, 1959.

WEBBS, E. J., CAMPBELL, D. T., SCHWARTZ, R. D. and SECHREST, L., *Unobtrusive Measures, Nonreactive Research in the Social Sciences*, Rand McNally, Chicago, 1966.

Chapter 3

References

1. BEEBE-CENTER, J. G., *The Psychology of Pleasantness*, Van Nostrand, London, 1966.

2. SHERIF, M., 'A study of some social factors in perception', *Arch. Psychol.*, No. 187, 1935 (cited in Reference 3).

3. SHERIF, M. and SHERIF, C. W., *Social Psychology*, Harper and Row, London, 1969.

4. GOMBRICH, E. H., *Art an Illusion: a study in the Psychology of Pictorial Representation*, Phaidon, London, 1960.

5. HOCHBERG, J. E., *Perception*, Prentice-Hall, Englewood Cliffs, N.J., 1964.

6. KÖHLER, W., *Principles of Gestalt Psychology*, Harcourt, New York, 1935.

7. STEVENS, S. S., 'On the psychophysical law', *Psychological Review*, **64**(3), 153–81 (1968).

8. STEVENS, S. S., 'To honour Fechner and repeal his law', *Science*, **133**, 80–6 (1961).

9. AMES, A., *Nature and Origins of Perceptions*, The Hanover Institute: Hanover, N.H., 1949.

10. OSGOOD, C. E., *Method and Theory in Experimental Psychology*, Oxford Press, New York, 1953 (*see* p. 263ff).

11. ITTELSON, W. H. (ed.) *Environment and Cognition*, Seminar Press, New York, 1973.

12. NAGASE, K., *A study of the correspondence between man and architecture*, M.Sc. Thesis, Hosei University, Tokyo, 1969.

13. MILLER, G. A., 'The magical number seven plus or minus two: some limits on our capacity for processing information', *Psychological Review*, **63**, 81–97 (1956).

14. HUNTER, I. M. L., *Memory*, Penguin, Harmondsworth, 1966.

15. BROADBENT, D. E., *Perception and Communication*, Pergamon, Oxford, 1964.

16. HEBB, D. O., 'Drives and the c.n.s. (conceptual nervous system)', *Psychological Review*, **62**, 243–54 (1955).

17. VERNON, J., *Inside the Blackroom*, Penguin, Harmondsworth, 1963.

18. JERISON, H. J., 'Activation and long term performances', in *Attention and Performance* (ed. A. F. Sanders) North Holland, Amsterdam, 1967.
19. CLARIDGE, G., CANTER, S. and HUME, W. I., *Personality Differences and Biological Variations: A Study of Twins*, Pergamon, Oxford, 1973.
20. BERLYNE, D. E., *Aesthetics and Psychobiology*, Appleton Century Crofts, New York, 1971.
21. VALENTINE, C. W., *The Experimental Psychology of Beauty*, Methuen, London, 1962.
22. EDGE, M. D., *A survey and evaluation of pythagorean influences in architecture*, M.A. Thesis, Liverpool University, 1957.
23. HALL, R., METCALFE, J., THORNE, R. and PURCELL, T., *A Preliminary Study of the Effect of Colour on Apparent Distance*, Architectural Psychology Research Unit, University of Sydney, Technical Report No. R: ME1, 1972.

Further Reading

BROADBENT, D. E., *Perception and Communication*, Pergamon, Oxford, 1964.
GIBSON, J. J., *The Senses Considered as Perceptual Systems*, Houghton-Miflin, New York, 1966.
GREGORY, R. L., *The Intelligent Eye*, Weidenfeld and Nicolson, London, 1970.
VERNON, M. D. (ed.) *Experiments in Visual Perception*, Penguin, Harmondsworth, 1970.
VALENTINE, C. W., *The Experimental Psychology of Beauty*, Methuen, London, 1962.

Chapter 4

References

1. TOLMAN, E. C., 'Cognitive maps in rats and men', *Psychological Review*, **53**, 189–208 (1948).
2. HULL, C. L., *Principles of Behaviour*, Appleton Century Crofts, New York, 1943.
3. MOWRER, O. H., *Learning Theory and Behaviour*, Wiley, New York, 1960.
4. GOLLEDGE, R. G. and SANNARAS, G., 'Cognitive approaches to the analysis of human spatial behaviour, in (ed. W. H. Ittelson) *Environment and Cognition*, Seminar Press, New York, 1973.
5. SKINNER, B. F., *Science and Human Behaviour*, Macmillan, New York, 1953.
6. PAVLOV, I. P., *Conditioned Reflexes*, Oxford University Press, London, 1927.
7. MOWRER, O. H., *Learning Theory and the Symbolic Processes*, Wiley, London, 1960.

Further Reading

BORGER, R. and SEABORNE, A. E. M., *The Psychology of Learning*, Penguin, Harmondsworth, 1966.
GAGNE, R. M., *The Conditions of Learning*, Holt, Rinehart and Winston, London, 1969.
HILGARD, E. R., *Theories of Learning*, Methuen, London, 1958.

Chapter 5

References

1. CANTER, D. V., 'Royal Hospital for Sick Children': a psychological analysis', *Architects' Journal*, 6 September 1972, pp. 525–64.
2. LINDHEIM, R., GLASER, H. H. and COFFIN, C., *Changing Hospital Environments for Children*, Harvard Press, Cambridge, Mass., 1972.
3. BROMLEY, D. B., *The Psychology of Human Ageing*, Penguin, Harmondsworth, 1966.
4. EISDORFER, C. and LAWTON, M. P. (eds.) *The Psychology of Adult Development and Ageing*, American Psychological Association, Washington, 1973.
5. LEE, T. R., 'Psychology and architectural determinism', *Architects' Journal*, 4th August, 253–62 (1971).
6. CLARIDGE, G., CANTER, S. and HUME, W. I., *Personality Differences and Biological Variations: A Study of Twins*, Pergamon, Oxford, 1973.
7. FLAVELL, J. H., *The Developmental Psychology of Jean Piaget*, Van Nostrand, London, 1963.
8. WALK, R. D. and GIBSON, E. J., 'A comparative and analytical study of visual depth perception', *Psychological Monographs*, **75**(15), 1–44 (1961).
9. WALK, R. D., 'The development of depth perceptions in animals and human infants', *Monographs of the Society for Research in Child Development*, **31**, 82–108 (1966).
10. FANTZ, R. L., 'The origin of form perception', *Scientific American*, **204**, 66–72 (1961).
11. HAITH, M. M., 'The response of the human newborn to visual movement', *Journal of Experimental Child Psychology*, **3**, 235–43 (1966).
12. SPEARS, W. C., 'Assessment of visual preference and discrimination in the four-month-old infant', *Journal of Comparative and Physiological Psychology*, **57**, 381–6 (1964).
13. HERSHENSON, M., 'Visual discrimination in the human newborn', *Journal of Comparative and Physiological Psychology*, **58**, 270–6 (1964).
14. FANTZ, R. L., 'Pattern discrimination and selective attention as determinants of perceptual development from birth', in *Perceptual Development in Children* (ed. A. H. Kidd and J. R. Rivoire), International Universities Press, London, 1966.
15. KARMEL, B. Z., 'The effects of age, complexity and amount of contour on pattern preferences in human infants', *Journal of Experimental Child Psychology'*, **7**, 339–54 (1969).
16. FANTZ, R. L. and NEVIS, S., 'Pattern preferences and perceptual-cognitive development in early infancy', *Merrill-Palmer Quarterly*, **13**, 77–108 (1967).
17. BRIAN, C. R. and GOODENOUGH, F. L., 'The relative potency of color and form perception at various ages', *Journal of Experimental Psychology*, **12**, 197–213 (1929).
18. CORAH, N. L., 'The influence of some stimulus characteristics on colour and form perception in nursery-school children', *Child Development*, **37**, 205–11 (1966).
19. KLEIN, S. D., *A developmental study of factual perception*, Unpublished Ph.D., Clark University, 1963.

20. PICK, H. L. and PICK, A. D., 'Sensory and perceptual development', in *Charmichael's Manual of Child Psychology* (ed. P. M. Mussen), Wiley, London, 1970.
21. BOWLBY, J., *Attachment and Loss: I. Attachment,* Penguin, Harmondsworth, 1972.
22. SHAFFER, H. R., *The Growth of Sociability,* Penguin, Harmondsworth, 1971.
23. HARLOW, H. F., 'The development of affectional patterns in infant monkeys', in *Determinants of Infant Behaviour* (ed. B. M. Foss), Methuen, London, 1961.
24. AINSWORTH, D. S. and WITTIG, B. A., 'Attachment and exploratory behaviour of one-year-olds in a strange situation', in *Determinants of Infant Behaviour,* Vol. 4 (ed. B. M. Foss), Methuen, London, 1969.

Further Reading

FOSS, B. M., *New Perspectives in Child Development,* Penguin, Harmondsworth, 1974.
FURTH, H. G., *Piaget and Knowledge,* Prentice-Hall, New Jersey, 1969.
NEWSON, J. and E., *Four Years Old in an Urban Community,* Penguin, Harmondsworth, 1969.
PIAGET, J. and INHELDER, B., *The Psychology of the Child,* Basic Books, New York, 1969.
SCHAFFER, H. R., *The Growth of Sociability,* Penguin, Harmondsworth, 1972.
STONE, L. J. and CHURCH, J., *Childhood and Adolescence: A Psychology of the Growing Person,* Random House, New York, 1973.

Chapter 6

References

1. OSGOOD, C. E., SUCI, G. J. and TANNEN BAUM, P. H., *The Measurement of Meaning,* University of Illinois, Urbana, 1957.
2. HARMAN, H. H., *Modern Factor Analysis,* University of Chicago, Chicago, 1960.
3. WARR, P. B. and KNAPPER, C., *The Perception of People and Events,* Wiley, London, 1968.
4. BUILDING PERFORMANCE RESEARCH UNIT, *Building Performance,* Applied Science Publishers, London, 1972.
5. OSGOOD, C. E., 'Interpersonal verbs and interpersonal behaviour', in *Studies in thought and language* (ed. J. L. Coward), University of Arizona, Tucson, 1970.
6. CANTER, D. V., *Evaluating Buildings: Emerging Scales and the Salience of Building Elements over Constructs,* Architectural Psychology Conference, Lund, June, 1973.
7. CANTER, D. V., *Scales for the Evaluation of Buildings,* Strathclyde University, Glasgow, 1971.
8. VIELHAUER, J. A., *The development of a semantic scale for the description of the physical environment,* Ph.D. Thesis, Louisiana State University, 1965.
9. HERSHBERGER, R. G., 'A study of meaning in architecture' in *EDRA* 1 (ed. M. Sanoff and S. Cohen), North Carolina State University, Raleigh, 1970.

10. CANTER, D. V. and WOOLS, R., 'A technique for the subjective appraisal of buildings', *Building Science*, 5(3 and 4) 187–98 (1970).
11. BUILDING PERFORMANCE RESEARCH UNIT, *Building Performance*, Applied Science Publishers, London, 1972.
12. CANTER, D. V. and THORNE, R., 'Attitudes to housing: a cross-cultural comparison', *Environment and Behaviour*, March, 3–31 (1972).
13. CANTER, D. V., SANCHEZ-ROBLES, J. and WATTS, N., *The Effects of Training and Culture on Evaluations of Houses*, Psychology and the Built Environment, conference, University of Surrey, September, 1973.
14. CANTER, D. V., 'An inter-group comparison of connotative dimensions in architecture', *Environment and Behaviour*, 1(1), 38–48 (1969).
15. KELLY, G. A., *The Psychology of Personal Constructs*, Norton, New York, 1955.
16. SLATER, P., *The Principal Components of a Repertory Grid*, Vincent Andrew, London, 1964.
17. BANNISTER, D. and MAIR, J. M. M., *The Evaluation of Personal Constructs*, Academic Press, London, 1968.
18. THOMAS, K. (ed.) *Attitudes and Behaviour*, Penguin, Harmondworth, 1973.

Further Reading

BANNISTER, D. and FRANSELLA, F., *Inquiring Man*, Penguin, Harmondsworth, 1971.
CHILD, D., *The Essentials of Factor Analysis*, Holt, Rinehart and Winston, London, 1970.
MULIAK, S. A., *The Foundations of Factor Analysis*, McGraw-Hill, New York, 1972.
SNIDER, J. G. and OSGOOD, C. E., *Semantic Differential Technique: A Sourcebook*, Aldine, Chicago, 1969.

Chapter 7

References

1. CHRISTIE, R. and GEIS, F. L., *Studies in Machiavellianism*, Academic Press, London, 1971.
2. HUTT, C., *Males and Females*, Penguin, Harmondworth, 1973.
3. BROMLEY, D. B., *Psychology of Human Ageing*, Penguin, Harmondsworth, 1966.
4. NEWSON, J. and E., *Four Years Old in an Urban Community*, Penguin, Harmondsworth, 1972.
5. WITKIN, H. A. *et al.*, *Psychological Differentiation: Studies of Development*, Wiley, London, 1962.
6. BANNISTER, D. and FRANSELLA, F., *Inquiring Man*, Penguin, Harmondsworth, 1971.
7. BARRON, F., 'Complexity-simplicity as a personality dimension', *Journal of Abnormal and Social Psychology*, 48(2), 163–72 (1953).
8. CANTER, D. V., 'Royal Hospital for Sick Children: A psychological analysis', *Architects' Journal*, 6 September, 525- 64 (1972).

9. CANTER, D., McCOMISKY, J. and JOHNSON, J., 'Familiarity with architectural concepts and academic achievement of architecture students', *Perceptual and Motor Skills*, **27**, 871–4 (1968).
10. BIERI, J. *et al.*, *Clinical and Social Judgement: The Discrimination of Behavioural Information*, Wiley, London, 1966.
11. EYSENCK, H. J. and EYSENCK, S. B. G., *Personality Structure and Measurement*, Routledge and Kegan Paul, London, 1969.
12. EYSEWICK, H. J., *The Biological Basis of Personality*, Charles C. Thomas, Illinois, 1967.
13. YERKES, R. M. and DODSON, J. D., 'The relation of strength of stimulus to rapidity of habit-formation', *Journal of Comparative and Neural Psychology*, **8**, 459–82 (1908). (Quoted in E. Duffy: *Activation and Behaviour*, Wiley, New York, 1962.)
14. CLARIDGE, G. S., *Personality and Arousal*, Pergamon, London, 1967.
15. WEISEN, A., *Differential Reinforcing Effects of Onset and Offset of Stimulation on the Operant Behaviour of Normals, Neurotics and Psychopaths*, Ph.D. Thesis, University of Florida, 1965 (Quoted in Reference 12).
16. HILL, A. R., 'Visibility and privacy', in *Architectural Psychology* (ed. D. Canter), *RIBA*, London, 1970.
17. BERLYNE, D. E., *Aesthetics and Psychobiology*, Appleton Century Crofts, New York, 1971.
18. KULLER, R., *Beyond Semantic Measurement*, Architectural Psychology Conference, Lund, June, 1973.

Further Reading

EYSENCK, H. J., *Fact and Fiction in Psychology*, Penguin, Harmondsworth, 1965.
LAZARUS, R. S. and OPTON, E. M. (eds.) *Personality*, Penguin, Harmondsworth, 1967.
SEMEONOFF, B. (ed.) *Personality Assessment*, Penguin, Harmondsworth, 1966.
WARR, P. B. (ed.) *Thought and Personality*, Penguin, Harmondsworth, 1970.

Chapter 8

References

1. MACARTHUR, R. H., 'Population ecology of some warblers of north-eastern coniferous forests', *Ecology*, **39**, 599–619 (1958).
2. KLOPFER, P. H., *Habitats and Territories: A Study of the Use of Space by Animals*, Basic Books, London, 1969.
3. HEDIGER, H., 'The evolution of territorial behaviour', in *The Social Life of Early Man* (ed. S. L. Washburn), Methuen, London, 1962.
4. STILITZ, I. B., 'Pedestrian congestion', in *Architectural Psychology*, (ed. D. Canter), *RIBA*, London, 1970.
5. KAMINO, K., *Studies of Pedestrian Movement*, Osaka University, Osaka, 1968.
6. HALL, E. T., *The Hidden Dimension*, Doubleday, New York, 1966.
7. SOMMER, R., *Personal Space: The Behavioural Basis of Design*, Prentice-Hall, Englewood Cliffs, N.J., 1969.

8. LEIBMAN, M., 'The effects of sex and race norms on personal space', *Environment and Behaviour*, **2**(2), 208–46 (1970).
9. LITTLE, K. B., 'Personal space', *Journal of Experimental Social Psychology*, **1**, 237–47 (1965).
10. ARGYLE, M. (ed.) *Social Encounters*, Penguin, Harmondsworth, 1973.
11. CANTER, D. V., 'Should we treat building users as subjects or objects', in *Architectural Psychology* (ed. D. Canter), *RIBA*, London, 1970.
12. SOMMER, R., 'Leadership and group geography', *Sociometry*, **24**, 99–109 (1961).
13. DELONG, A. J., 'Dominance-territorial relations in a small group', *Environment and Behaviour*, **2**(2), 179–91 (1970).
14. LIPMAN, A., 'Building design and social interaction', *Architects' Journal*, **147**, 23–30 (1968).
15. ARAKI, H., *The Ecology of Old People*, Japanese Institute of Architects Annual Conference, Tokyo, 1966.
16. ALTMAN, I., 'An ecological approach to the functioning of small social groups', in *Individual and Group Behaviour in Isolation* (ed. J. E. Rasmussen), Aldine, Chicago, 1971.
17. FESTINGER, L., SCHACTER, S. and BACK, K., *Social Pressures in Informal Groups*, Harper, New York, 1950.
18. MORENO, J. L., *Sociometry and the Science of Man*, Beacon House, New York, 1956.
19. CAREY, L. and MAPES, R., *The Sociology of Planning: A Study of Social Activity on New Housing Estates*, Batsford, London, 1971.
20. WELLS, B. W. P., 'The psycho-social influence of the building environment', *Building Science*, **1**, 153–65 (1965).
21. GULLAHORN, J. T., 'Distance and friendship as factors in the gross interaction matrix', *Sociometry*, **15**, 123–4 (1952).
22. PORTER, E. R., ARGYLE, M. and SALTER, V., 'What is signalled by proximity', *Perceptual and Motor Skills*, **30**, 39–42 (1970).

Further Reading

The above references cover most of the available introductory books, especially 2, 6, 7, 17 and 19.

Chapter 9

References

1. ROETHLISBERGER, F. J. and DICKSON, W. J., *Management and the Worker*, Harvard Press, Cambridge, Mass., 1939.
2. LANDSBERGER, H. A., *Hawthorn Revisited*, Cornell University, 1961.
3. BUILDING PERFORMANCE RESEARCH UNIT, *Building Performance*, Applied Science Publishers, London, 1972.
4. WHERRY, R. J., 'Factor analysis of morale data: reliability and validity', *Personnel Psychology*, **11**, 78–94 (1958).
5. HULIN, C. L. and SMITH, P. C., 'A linear model of job satisfaction', *Journal of Applied Psychology*, **49**(3), 209–16 (1965).

6. VAN ZELST, R. H., 'Validation of a sociometric regrouping procedure', *Journal of Abnormal and Social Psychology,* **47,** 299–301 (1952).
7. MORSE, N. C., *Satisfaction in the White-collar Job,* University of Michigan, Ann Arbor, 1953.
8. ARGYRIS, C., *Integrating the Individual and the Organisation,* Wiley, London, 1964.
9. BLAI, B., 'An occupational study of job satisfaction and need satisfaction', *Journal of Experimental Education,* **32**(4), 383–8 (1964).
10. HERZBERG, F., MAUSNER, B. and SNYDERMAN, B. B., *The Motivation to Work,* Chapman and Hall, London, 1962.
11. MARCH, J. G. and SIMON, H. A., *Organisation,* Wiley, New York, 1958.
12. LEAVITT, H. J., 'Some effects of certain communication patterns on group performance', *Journal of Abnormal and Social Psychology,* **46,** 38–50 (1951).
13. KLEIN, J., *The Study of Groups,* Routledge and Kegan Paul, London, 1956.
14. GIBBS, C. A. (ed.) *Leadership: Selected Readings,* Penguin, Harmondsworth, 1969.

Further Reading

BASS, B. M., *Organizational Psychology,* Allyn and Bacon, Boston, 1965.
SCHEIN, E. H., *Organizational Psychology,* Prentice-Hall, Englewood Cliffs, N.J., 1965.

Chapter 10

References

1. ROETHLISBERGER, F. J. and DICKSON, W. J., *Management and the Worker,* Harvard Press, Cambridge, Mass., 1939.
2. WYON, D. P., 'Studies of children under imposed noise and heat stress', *Ergonomics,* **13**(5), 598–612 (1970).
3. DEMOS, G. D. and ZUWAYLIF, F. H., *Windowless Classrooms Study,* Palm Springs Unified School District, California, 1967.

Index